Basic Computation Series 2000

Understanding Fractions

Loretta M. Taylor, Ed. D.

Harold D. Taylor, Ed. D.

Executive Editor: Catherine Anderson

Project Editor: ToniAnn Guadagnoli

Development Editor: Deborah J. Slade

Production/Manufacturing Director: Janet Yearian

Sr. Production/Manufacturing Coordinator: Roxanne Knoll

Design Director: Phyllis Aycock

Design Manager: Jeff Kelly

Cover Designer: Monika Popowitz

Interior Designer: Christy Butterfield

Composition: Alan Noyes

ISBN 0-7690-0115-7
Printed in the United States of America
4 5 6 7 8 9 10   06 05 04 03

1-800-321-3106
www.pearsonlearning.com

Dale Seymour Publications

Pearson Learning Group

Authors of the Basic Computation Series 2000

Loretta M. Taylor is a retired high school mathematics teacher. During her teaching career, she taught at Hillsdale High School in San Mateo, California; Crestmoor High School in San Bruno, California; Patterson High School in Patterson, California; Round Valley Union High School in Covelo, California; and Farmington High School in Farmington, New Mexico. Dr. Taylor obtained a B.S. in mathematics from Southeastern Oklahoma State University, and both an M.A. in mathematics and an Ed.D. in mathematics education from the University of Northern Colorado. She has been active in professional organizations at the local, state, and national levels, including the National Council of Teachers of Mathematics, the California Mathematics Council, the National Education Association, and the California Teachers Association. She has given a variety of talks and workshops at numerous conferences, schools, and universities. Dr. Taylor is a member of Lambda Sigma Tau, a national honorary science fraternity, and is coauthor of *Paper and Scissors Polygons and More, Algebra Book 1, Algebra Book 2,* and *Developing Skills in Algebra 1.* In retirement, she continues to be an active mathematics author and is involved with community organizations.

Harold D. Taylor is a retired high school mathematics teacher, having taught at Aragon High School in San Mateo, California; as well as at Patterson High School in Patterson, California; Round Valley Union High School in Covelo, California; and Farmington High School in Farmington, New Mexico. He has served in high schools not only as a mathematics teacher, but also as a mathematics department head and as an assistant principal. He received a B.S. in mathematics from Southeastern Oklahoma State University, and both an M.A. in mathematics and an Ed.D. in mathematics education from the University of Northern Colorado. Dr. Taylor has been very active in a number of professional organizations, having worked in a variety of significant capacities for the National Council of Teachers of Mathematics and the California Mathematics Council. He was chairman of the Publicity and Information Committee and the Local Organizing Committee for the Fourth International Congress on Mathematics Education at Berkeley, California, was on the writing team of the California Assessment Test, and was a member of the California State Mathematics Framework and Criteria Committee, chairing the California State Mathematics Framework Addendum Committee. Since 1966, he has spoken at more than one hundred local, state, and national meetings on mathematics and mathematics education. Dr. Taylor is author of *Ten Mathematics Projects and Career Education Infusion,* and coauthor of *Algebra Book 1, Algebra Book 2,* and *Developing Skills in Algebra 1.* In 1989 he was the California recipient of the Presidential Award for Excellence in Teaching Secondary Mathematics. In retirement, Dr. Taylor is continuing to produce mathematics materials for the classroom, and also serves his community as County Judge in Custer County, Colorado, having been appointed to this position by Governor Roy Romer.

Table of Contents

A Note of Introduction

To the Teacher

Some students are familiar with computational work but have never really mastered it. Perhaps this is the result of a lack of practice. With the *Basic Computation Series 2000,* you can provide students with as much practice as they need. You can teach, check up, reteach, and reinforce. You can give classwork and homework. If you wish, you can create a full year's course in basic computation, or you can provide skills maintenance when it's needed. All the work is here. Select the pages you want to use for the students who need them.

To the Student

You can't play a guitar before you learn the chords. You can't shoot a hook shot before you learn the lay-up. You can't pass a mathematics exam before you learn to compute, and you can't master computational skills until you learn the mathematical facts and procedures. Learning takes practice; there are no shortcuts. The pages in this book are for practice. Do your math every day and think about what you're doing. If you don't understand something, ask questions. Don't do too much work in your head; it's worth an extra sheet of paper to write down your steps. Also, be patient with yourself. Learning takes time.

Although calculators and other computational devices are readily available to most everyone, you will be forever handicapped if you are not able to perform basic mathematical computations without the aid of a mechanical or electronic computational device. Learn and master the procedures so that you can rely on your own abilities.

To the Parent

The importance of the development of mathematical skills cannot be emphasized enough. Mathematics is needed to estimate materials for a construction job or to price a car. It's needed to predict earthquakes and to prescribe medicine. It helps you determine how to stretch your dollars and pay your bills. This program provides the practice students need to develop the essential computational skills. Conventional algorithms are utilized throughout the *Basic Computation Series 2000.* You can help your children learn these skills. Give them your support and encouragement. Urge them to do their homework. Be there to answer questions. Give them a quiet place to work. Make them feel good about trying. Your help can make the difference.

About the Program

What is the Basic Computation Series 2000?

The books in the *Basic Computation Series 2000* provide comprehensive practice in all the essential computational skills. There are nine practice books and a test book. The practice books consist of carefully sequenced drill worksheets organized in groups of five. The test book contains daily quizzes (160 quizzes in all), semester tests, and year-end tests written in standardized-test formats.

Book 1	Working with Whole Numbers
Book 2	Understanding Fractions
Book 3	Working with Fractions
Book 4	Working with Decimals
Book 5	Working with Percents
Book 6	Understanding Measurement
Book 7	Working with Perimeter and Area
Book 8	Working with Surface Area and Volume
Book 9	Applying Computational Skills
Test Book 10	Basic Computation Quizzes and Tests

Who can use the Basic Computation Series 2000?

The *Basic Computation Series 2000* is appropriate for use by any person, young or old, who has not achieved computational proficiency. It may be used with any program calling for carefully sequenced computational practice. The material is especially suitable for use with students in fifth grade, middle school, junior high school, special education classes, and high school. It may be used by classroom teachers, substitute teachers, tutors, and parents. It is also useful for those in adult education or those preparing for the General Education Development Test (GED), and for others wishing to study on their own.

What is in this book?

This book is a practice book. In addition to explanation and examples for the student, parent, and teacher, it contains student worksheets, answers, and a record sheet.

Worksheets

The worksheets are designed to give even the slowest student a chance to master the essential computational skills. Most worksheets come in five equivalent forms allowing for pre-testing, practice, and post-testing on any particular skill. Each set of worksheets provides practice on only one or two specific skills and the work progresses in very small steps from one set to the next. Instructions are clear and simple. Ample practice is provided on each page, giving students the opportunity to strengthen their skills. Answers to each problem are included in back of the book.

Explanatory Material

The beginning of each section includes explanatory material designed to help students, parents, and teachers understand the material in the section and its purpose. Fully-worked examples show how to work each type of exercise. The example solutions are written in a straightforward manner so as to be easily understood.

Student Record Sheet

A record sheet is provided to help in recording progress and assessing instructional needs.

Answers

Answers to all problems are included in the back of the book.

How can the Basic Computation Series 2000 be used?

The materials in the *Basic Computation Series 2000* can serve as the major skeleton of a skills program or as supplements to any other computational skills program. The large number of worksheets provides a wide variety from which to choose and allows flexibility in structuring a program to meet individual needs. The following suggestions are offered to show how the *Basic Computation Series 2000* may be adapted to a particular situation.

Minimal Competency Practice

In various fields and schools, standardized tests are used for entrance, passage from one level to another, and certification of competency or proficiency prior to graduation. The materials in the *Basic Computation Series 2000* are particularly well-suited to preparing for any of the various mathematics competency tests, including the mathematics portion of the General Educational Development test (GED) used to certify high school equivalency.

Together, the books in the *Basic Computation Series 2000* provide practice in all the essential computational skills measured on competency tests. The semester tests and year-end tests from the test book are written in standardized-test format. These tests can be used as sample minimal competency tests. The worksheets can be used to brush up on skills measured by the competency tests.

Skills Maintenance

Since most worksheets come in five equivalent forms, the work can be organized into weekly units as suggested by the following schedule: A five-day schedule can begin on any day of the week. The authors' ideal schedule begins on Thursday, with reteaching on Friday. Monday and Tuesday are for practice touch-up teaching, reinforcing, and individualized instruction. Wednesday is test day. Daily quizzes from the *Basic Computation Quizzes* and *Tests Book* can be used on the drill-and-practice days for maintenance of previously-learned skills or diagnosis of skill deficiencies. Ideally, except for test days, a quiz may be given during the first fifteen minutes of a class period with the remainder of the period used for instruction and practice with other materials.

Authors' Suggested Teaching Schedule

	Day 1	Day 2	Day 3	Day 4	Day 5
Week 1	Pages 6 and 7 Pages 16 and 17	Pages 8 and 9 Pages 18 and 19	Pages 10 and 11 Pages 20 and 21	Pages 12 and 13 Pages 22 and 23	Pages 14 and 15 Pages 24 and 25
Week 2	Pages 26 and 27 Pages 36 and 37	Pages 28 and 29 Pages 38 and 39	Pages 30 and 31 Pages 40 and 41	Pages 32 and 33 Pages 42 and 43	Pages 34 and 35 Pages 44 and 45
Week 3	Pages 49 and 50 Pages 59 and 60	Pages 51 and 52 Pages 61 and 62	Pages 53 and 54 Pages 63 and 64	Pages 55 and 56 Pages 65 and 66	Pages 57 and 58 Pages 67 and 68
Week 4	Pages 75 and 76 Pages 85 and 86	Pages 77 and 78 Pages 87 and 88	Pages 79 and 80 Pages 89 and 90	Pages 81 and 82 Pages 91 and 92	Pages 83 and 84 Pages 93 and 94
Week 5	Pages 95 and 96	Pages 97 and 98	Pages 99 and 100	Pages 101 and 102	Pages 103 and 104

Supplementary Drill

There are more than 18,000 problems in the *Basic Computation Series 2000*. When students need more practice with a given skill, use the appropriate worksheets from the series. They are suitable for classwork or homework practice following the teaching of a specific skill. With five equivalent pages for most worksheets, adequate practice is provided for each essential skill.

How are the materials prepared?

The books are designed with pages that can be easily reproduced. Permanent transparencies can be produced using a copy machine and special transparencies designed for this purpose. The program will run more smoothly if the student's work is stored in folders. Record sheets can be attached to the folders so that students, teachers, or parents can keep records of an individual's progress. Materials stored in this way are readily available for conferences with the student or parent.

Student Record Sheet

Worksheets Completed

Page Number

6	8	10	12		14
7	9	11	13		15
16	18	20	22		24
17	19	21	23		25
26	28	30	32		34
27	29	31	33		35
36	38	40	42		44
37	39	41	43		45
49	51	53	55		57
50	52	54	56		58
59	61	63	65		67
60	62	64	66		68
75	77	79	81		83
76	78	80	82		84
85	87	89	91		93
86	88	90	92		94
95	97	99	101		103
96	98	100	102		104

Quiz Grades

No.	Score

Checklist

Skill Mastered	Date
❏ fractional parts	
❏ equivalent fractions	
❏ reducing fractions	
❏ proportions	
❏ word problems	
❏ least common denominator	
❏ ordering fractions	
❏ improper fractions to mixed numbers	
❏ mixed numbers to improper fractions	
❏ simplifying mixed numbers	
❏ reading decimal numbers	
❏ writing decimal numbers	
❏ number line graphs	
❏ fractions to decimals	
❏ decimals to fractions	

Notes

Common Fractions, Equivalent Fractions, and Ratio and Proportion

Whole numbers and operations on whole numbers were explored in Book 1, *Working With Whole Numbers*. However, the study of numbers is not complete without the study of *fractions*. Fractions indicate parts of whole numbers. Three types of fractions are explored in this series: common fractions, decimal numbers, and percents. There are three types of common fractions: proper fractions, improper fractions, and mixed numbers. The first part of this book will be devoted to learning about proper fractions.

A proper common fraction is written with a numerator and a denominator, separated by a line called a *fraction bar*. In a proper fraction, the numerator is a smaller number than the denominator. The denominator denotes the number of parts into which the whole is divided; the numerator denotes the number of these parts being considered. The numerator is written above or to the left of the fraction bar; the denominator is written below or to the right of the fraction bar. For example, in the fraction $\frac{1}{2}$ (sometimes written 1/2) the numerator is 1 and the denominator, 2. This fraction represents 1 of the 2 parts into which a whole has been divided.

Example 1:   What fractional part of the circles to the right contain X's?   ⊗ ⊗ ○ ○ ○

Solution: Of the five circles shown, 2 of them contain X's. The fraction $\frac{2}{5}$ indicates the fractional part of the circles that contain X's.

Example 2:   The distance from A to B is what fractional part of the distance from A to C?

```
├───────┼───────┼───────┼───────┤
A       B                       C
```

Solution: The distance from A to C is divided into four equal parts. The distance from A to B is one of these parts. Therefore, the distance from A to B is $\frac{1}{4}$ of the distance from A to C.

Example 3:   The shaded part of the figure below is what part of the whole figure?

Solution: The figure is divided into eight equal parts, three of which are shaded. Therefore, the shaded part is $\frac{3}{8}$ of the whole figure.

Basic Computation Series 2000: Understanding Fractions
SECTION 1 Common Fractions, Equivalent Fractions, and Ratio and Proportion

1

Copyright © Dale Seymour Publications®

Example 4:   **a.** Seven cents is what part of a dollar?

b. Twenty-three cents is what part of a dollar?

c. Eighty-one cents is what part of a dollar?

Solution: A dollar is divided into one hundred equal parts, each of which is a cent.

a. Seven cents is $\frac{7}{100}$ of a dollar.

b. Twenty-three cents is $\frac{23}{100}$ of a dollar.

c. Eighty-one cents is $\frac{81}{100}$ of a dollar.

Equivalent fractions are different fractions that represent the same number. If a whole is divided into three parts, one part represents $\frac{1}{3}$ of the whole. If a whole is divided into six parts, two parts represent $\frac{2}{6}$ of the whole. By studying the figures at the right, it can be seen that $\frac{1}{3}$ and $\frac{2}{6}$ represent the same amount and are, therefore, equivalent fractions.

$\frac{1}{3}$ is shaded

$\frac{2}{6}$ is shaded

A fraction equivalent to a given fraction can be generated by multiplying both the numerator and denominator of the fraction by the same non-zero number. A fraction equivalent to a given fraction can also be generated by dividing the numerator and denominator by the same non-zero number.

Example 5:   Write three fractions equivalent to $\frac{1}{2}$. (Note: An infinite number of such fractions can be written.)

Solution: Multiply the numerator and denominator of $\frac{1}{2}$ by 4, 7, and 13. (The choice of 4, 7, and 13 is arbitrary; any numbers except zero can be used.)

$$1 \times 4 = 4 \qquad 1 \times 7 = 7 \qquad 1 \times 13 = 13$$
$$2 \times 4 = 8 \qquad 2 \times 7 = 14 \qquad 2 \times 13 = 26$$

Thus, $\frac{4}{8}$, $\frac{7}{14}$, and $\frac{13}{26}$ are each equivalent to $\frac{1}{2}$.

Example 6:   Write a fraction equivalent to $\frac{5}{8}$ that has a denominator of 24.

Solution: To get a denominator of 24, 8 must be multiplied by 3. Therefore, to get the desired fraction that is equivalent to $\frac{5}{8}$, multiply the numerator, 5, by the same number, 3. The result is 15. Thus, $\frac{15}{24}$ is equivalent to $\frac{5}{8}$.

A fraction is considered *reduced to lowest terms* if the greatest common factor (GCF) of the numerator and denominator is 1. (Note: The concept of *greatest common factor* is explored in Book 1.)

Basic Computation Series 2000: Understanding Fractions
SECTION 1 Common Fractions, Equivalent Fractions, and Ratio and Proportion

2

Example 7: Reduce each of the following fractions to lowest terms.

    a. $\frac{10}{20}$

    b. $\frac{26}{39}$

    c. $\frac{42}{56}$

    d. $\frac{30}{66}$

Solution: Write the numerator and denominator of each fraction in prime factored form and determine the GCF of each. Then divide the numerator and denominator of each fraction by that GCF.

    a. $10 = 2 \times 5$; $20 = 2 \times 2 \times 5$. The GCF of 10 and 20 is 2×5, or 10. Divide both the numerator and denominator by 10. $\frac{10}{20} = \frac{1}{2}$

    b. $26 = 2 \times 13$; $39 = 3 \times 13$. The GCF of 26 and 39 is 13. Divide both the numerator and denominator by 13. $\frac{26}{39} = \frac{2}{3}$

    c. $42 = 2 \times 3 \times 7$; $56 = 2 \times 2 \times 2 \times 7$. The GCF of 42 and 56 is 2×7, or 14. Divide both the numerator and denominator by 14. $\frac{42}{56} = \frac{3}{4}$

    d. $30 = 2 \times 3 \times 5$;. $66 = 2 \times 3 \times 11$. The GCF of 30 and 66 is 2×3, or 6. Divide both the numerator and denominator by 6. $\frac{30}{66} = \frac{5}{11}$

Example 8: Replace the ? to make equivalent fractions.

    a. $\frac{4}{5} = \frac{?}{20}$

    b. $\frac{3}{8} = \frac{?}{48}$

    c. $\frac{1}{3} = \frac{?}{33}$

    d. $\frac{5}{6} = \frac{?}{30}$

Solution: Decide what the first denominator was multiplied by to get the second denominator. This can be determined by dividing the second denominator by the first. Then multiply the given numerator by the multiplier.

    a. $20 \div 5 = 4$. Multiply 4 by 4.

$$\frac{4}{5} = \frac{16}{20}$$

    b. $48 \div 8 = 6$. Multiply 3 by 6.

$$\frac{3}{8} = \frac{18}{48}$$

Basic Computation Series 2000: Understanding Fractions
SECTION 1 Common Fractions, Equivalent Fractions, and Ratio and Proportion

3

c. $33 \div 3 = 11$. Multiply 1 by 11.

$$\frac{1}{3} = \frac{11}{33}$$

d. $30 \div 6 = 5$. Multiply 5 by 5.

$$\frac{5}{6} = \frac{25}{30}$$

Example 9:   Complete each of the following.

   a. Fifteen cents is _____ of $1. (Reduce to lowest terms.)

   b. _____ cents is $\frac{3}{5}$ of a dollar.

Solution: **a.** Since a dollar has 100 equal parts, each of which is a cent, 15 cents is $\frac{15}{100}$ of a dollar. Since $15 = 3 \times 5$ and $100 = 2^2 \times 5^2$, the GCF of 15 and 100 is 5. To reduce, divide the numerator and denominator of $\frac{15}{100}$ by 5. Fifteen cents is $\frac{3}{20}$ of $1.

   b. Write $\frac{3}{5}$ as a fraction with a denominator of 100. Since $100 \div 5 = 20$, multiply the numerator, 3, by 20 to get the desired equivalent fraction with denominator 100. 60 cents is $\frac{3}{5}$ of a dollar.

One way of comparing numbers involves subtraction and indicates how much larger one number is than another. A *ratio* is another way of comparing numbers and uses division rather than subtraction. Consider the numbers 12 and 2. Comparing these two numbers by subtraction gives a difference of 10. Comparing these numbers by division gives a ratio of 6 to 1; that is, 12 and 2 are, respectively, 6 and 1 times the same number, 2. In the same way, the ratio of 2 to 12 can be written $\frac{2}{12}$ which equals $\frac{1}{6}$. The ratio "two to three" is written $\frac{2}{3}$ and looks exactly like the fraction that is read "two thirds." The arithmetic of ratios is exactly the same as the arithmetic of fractions; there is no difference. Equivalent ratios can be determined using the same method used to determine equivalent fractions.

If two ratios are equal they form a *proportion*. Many problems can be solved by using proportions. In a proportion, the *cross products* are equal. The cross products are found by multiplying the denominator of each fraction by the numerator of the other. For example, in the proportion $\frac{2}{3} = \frac{4}{6}$, the cross products are 2×6 and 3×4. In this case, the cross products equal 12. If the cross products are not equal, the ratios are not equal ($\neq$). For example, consider the ratios $\frac{5}{8}$ and $\frac{2}{3}$. The cross products, 15 and 16, are not equal; therefore, $\frac{5}{8} \neq \frac{2}{3}$.

Basic Computation Series 2000: Understanding Fractions
SECTION 1 Common Fractions, Equivalent Fractions, and Ratio and Proportion

Example 10: Use cross products to replace the ? with = or ≠ to make a true statement.

　　　　a. $\frac{7}{11}$? $\frac{77}{121}$

　　　　b. $\frac{3}{4}$? $\frac{6}{12}$

Solution: **a.** To find the cross products, multiply 7×121 to get the product 847 and 11×77 to get the product 847. Since the cross products are equal, the ratios are equal. Thus, $\frac{7}{11} = \frac{77}{121}$.

　　　　b. To find the cross products multiply 3×12 to get 36, and 4 times 6 to get 24. The cross products are not equal, therefore the ratios are not equal. Thus, $\frac{3}{4} \neq \frac{6}{12}$.

Example 11: If an automobile travels 378 miles in 9 hours, how far would it travel in 27 hours at the same rate?

Solution: This problem can be solved by using ratios. The rate of travel is 378 miles to 9 hours, a ratio of 378 to 9. Write a fraction equivalent to $\frac{378}{9}$ that has a denominator of 27; that is, $\frac{378}{9} = \frac{?}{27}$. The denominator of the second fraction is 3 times the denominator of the first fraction. To get the numerator of the second fraction, multiply the numerator of the first fraction by 3. $378 \times 3 = 1,134$. Thus, the automobile would travel 1,134 miles in 27 hours.

Basic Computation Series 2000: Understanding Fractions
SECTION 1 Common Fractions, Equivalent Fractions, and Ratio and Proportion

5

Fractional Parts

Complete each of the following.

		number of circles with X's	total number of circles	fraction of circles with X's
1.	⊗ ⊗ ⊗ ○ ○	3	5	$\frac{3}{5}$
2.	⊗ ○ ○ ○ ○ ○	_____	_____	_____
3.	⊗ ⊗ ⊗ ⊗ ⊗ ○ ○ ○	_____	_____	_____
4.	⊗ ⊗ ⊗ ○ ○ ○ ○	_____	_____	_____
5.	⊗ ○ ○ ○ ○ ○ ○ ○	_____	_____	_____
6.	⊗ ⊗ ⊗ ○ ○ ○ ○ ○	_____	_____	_____
7.	⊗ ⊗ ○ ○ ○ ○ ○ ○ ○	_____	_____	_____
8.	⊗ ⊗ ⊗ ⊗ ⊗ ⊗ ⊗ ○	_____	_____	_____
9.	⊗ ⊗ ⊗ ⊗ ⊗ ○	_____	_____	_____
10.	⊗ ⊗ ⊗ ⊗ ⊗ ○ ○ ○ ○	_____	_____	_____

From A to B is what fractional part of the distance from A to C?

11. $\frac{1}{2}$

12. 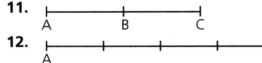 _____

13. 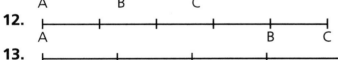 _____

14. 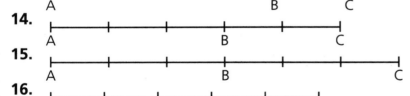 _____

15. _____

16. _____

17. _____

18. _____

19. _____

20. 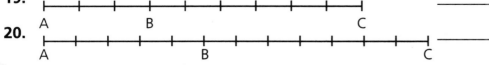 _____

Basic Computation Series 2000: Understanding Fractions
SECTION 1 Common Fractions, Equivalent Fractions, and Ratio and Proportion

Fractional Parts

Name the fractional part of each figure that is shaded.

1. $\frac{1}{3}$

6. _____

2. _____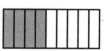

7. _____

3. _____

8. _____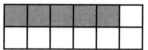

4. _____

9. _____

5. _____

10. _____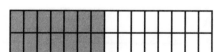

Complete each of the following.

11. Twenty-five cents is $\frac{1}{4}$ of $1.

12. Ten cents is _____ of $0.25.

13. Five cents is _____ of $0.10.

14. _____ cents is $\frac{2}{5}$ of a dollar.

15. _____ cents is $\frac{1}{2}$ of a dollar.

16. _____ dollars is $\frac{3}{10}$ of ten dollars.

Basic Computation Series 2000: Understanding Fractions
SECTION 1 Common Fractions, Equivalent Fractions, and Ratio and Proportion

7

Fractional Parts

Complete each of the following.

		number of circles with X's	total number of circles	fraction of circles with X's

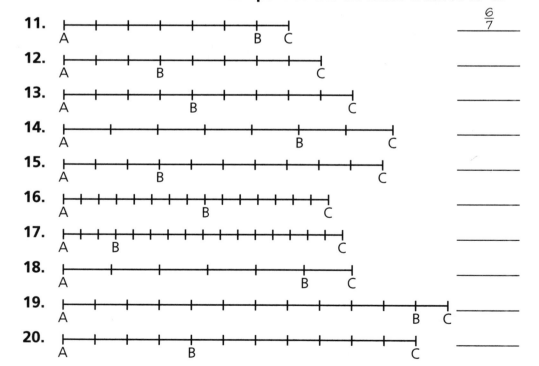

1. ⊗ ⊗ ○ ○ ○ · 2 · 5 · $\frac{2}{5}$

2. ⊗ ⊗ ⊗ ⊗ ⊗ ○ · _____ · _____ · _____

3. ⊗ ⊗ ⊗ ⊗ ⊗ ○ ○ ○ ○ · _____ · _____ · _____

4. ⊗ ⊗ ⊗ ○ · _____ · _____ · _____

5. ⊗ ⊗ ⊗ ⊗ ⊗ ⊗ ⊗ ○ ○ ○ · _____ · _____ · _____

6. ⊗ ⊗ ○ ○ ○ ○ ○ · _____ · _____ · _____

7. ⊗ ○ ○ · _____ · _____ · _____

8. ⊗ ⊗ ⊗ ⊗ ⊗ ○ ○ ○ · _____ · _____ · _____

9. ⊗ ⊗ ⊗ ⊗ ⊗ ○ ○ · _____ · _____ · _____

10. ⊗ ○ ○ ○ ○ ○ ○ ○ ○ · _____ · _____ · _____

From A to B is what fractional part of the distance from A to C?

11. $\frac{6}{7}$

12.   _____

13.   _____

14.   _____

15.   _____

16.   _____

17.   _____

18.   _____

19.   _____

20.   _____

Fractional Parts

Name the fractional part of each figure that is shaded.

1. $\frac{5}{10}$ or $\frac{1}{2}$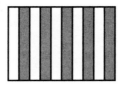

2. _____

3. _____

4. _____

5. _____

6. _____

7. _____

8. _____

9. _____

10. _____

Complete each of the following.

11. Fifty cents is __$\frac{1}{2}$__ of $1.

12. Five cents is _____ of $1.

13. One dollar is _____ of $5.

14. _____ cents is $\frac{3}{4}$ of a dollar.

15. _____ cents is $\frac{1}{10}$ of a dollar.

16. _____ dollars is $\frac{4}{5}$ of five dollars.

Basic Computation Series 2000: Understanding Fractions
SECTION 1 Common Fractions, Equivalent Fractions, and Ratio and Proportion

9

Fractional Parts

Complete each of the following.

		number of circles with X's	total number of circles	fraction of circles with X's
1.	⊗ ⊗ ⊗ ⊗ ○ ○ ○	4	7	4/7
2.	⊗ ⊗ ⊗ ○	_____	_____	_____
3.	⊗ ⊗ ⊗ ⊗ ⊗ ⊗ ○	_____	_____	_____
4.	⊗ ⊗ ⊗ ⊗ ⊗ ○ ○ ○	_____	_____	_____
5.	⊗ ⊗ ⊗ ○ ○ ○ ○ ○ ○	_____	_____	_____
6.	⊗ ⊗ ⊗ ○ ○ ○ ○ ○	_____	_____	_____
7.	⊗ ⊗ ⊗ ⊗ ⊗ ⊗ ⊗ ○ ○	_____	_____	_____
8.	⊗ ⊗ ⊗ ⊗ ⊗ ⊗ ⊗ ○	_____	_____	_____
9.	⊗ ⊗ ○ ○ ○ ○ ○ ○	_____	_____	_____
10.	⊗ ⊗ ⊗ ○ ○	_____	_____	_____

From A to B is what fractional part of the distance from A to C?

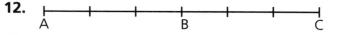

11. $\frac{3}{8}$

12. _____

13. _____

14. _____

15. _____

16. _____

17. _____

18. _____

19. _____

20. _____

Basic Computation Series 2000: Understanding Fractions
SECTION 1 Common Fractions, Equivalent Fractions, and Ratio and Proportion

Fractional Parts

Name the fractional part of each figure that is shaded.

1. $\frac{1}{4}$

2. _____

3. _____

4. _____

5. _____

6. _____

7. _____

8. _____

9. _____

10. _____

Complete each of the following.

11. Ten cents is $\frac{1}{10}$ of $1.

12. Fifty cents is _____ of $5.

13. Five cents is _____ of $0.25.

14. _____ cents is $\frac{1}{2}$ of a dollar.

15. _____ cents is $\frac{1}{5}$ of a dollar.

16. _____ dollars is $\frac{2}{5}$ of ten dollars.

Basic Computation Series 2000: Understanding Fractions
SECTION 1 Common Fractions, Equivalent Fractions, and Ratio and Proportion

11

Fractional Parts

Complete each of the following.

		number of circles with X's	total number of circles	fraction of circles with X's
1.	⊗⊗⊗⊗⊗⊗⊗○	7	8	$\frac{7}{8}$
2.	⊗⊗○○○○○	_____	_____	_____
3.	⊗⊗⊗⊗⊗○	_____	_____	_____
4.	○○○○○○○○○	_____	_____	_____
5.	⊗⊗⊗⊗⊗○○○	_____	_____	_____
6.	⊗⊗○	_____	_____	_____
7.	⊗⊗⊗⊗⊗○○○	_____	_____	_____
8.	⊗⊗⊗⊗⊗⊗⊗⊗⊗○	_____	_____	_____
9.	⊗⊗⊗⊗⊗○○	_____	_____	_____
10.	⊗⊗○○○○○○	_____	_____	_____

From A to B is what fractional part of the distance from A to C?

11. $\frac{1}{2}$

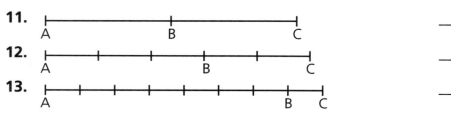

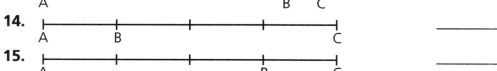

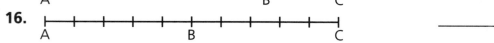

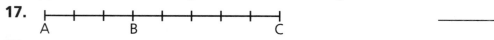

12. _____
13. _____
14. _____
15. _____
16. _____
17. _____
18. _____
19. _____
20. _____

Fractional Parts

Name the fractional part of each figure that is shaded.

1. $\frac{1}{4}$

2. _____

3. _____

4. _____

5. _____

6. _____

7. _____

8. _____

9. _____

10. _____

Complete each of the following.

11. Twenty cents is ___$\frac{1}{5}$___ of $1.

12. Ten cents is _____ of $5.

13. Twenty five cents is _____ of $0.50.

14. _____ cents is $\frac{1}{4}$ of a dollar.

15. _____ cents is $\frac{3}{5}$ of a dollar.

16. _____ dollars is $\frac{2}{5}$ of five dollars.

Basic Computation Series 2000: Understanding Fractions
SECTION 1 Common Fractions, Equivalent Fractions, and Ratio and Proportion

13

Fractional Parts

Complete each of the following.

		number of circles with X's	total number of circles	fraction of circles with X's
1.	⊗ ⊗ ⊗ ○	3	4	$\frac{3}{4}$
2.	⊗ ⊗ ⊗ ○ ○ ○ ○ ○	_____	_____	_____
3.	⊗ ⊗ ⊗ ⊗ ⊗ ⊗ ⊗ ⊗ ○	_____	_____	_____
4.	⊗ ⊗ ⊗ ⊗ ○ ○ ○	_____	_____	_____
5.	⊗ ⊗ ⊗ ⊗ ○ ○ ○ ○ ○	_____	_____	_____
6.	⊗ ⊗ ○	_____	_____	_____
7.	⊗ ⊗ ⊗ ⊗ ⊗ ⊗ ⊗ ○	_____	_____	_____
8.	⊗ ⊗ ⊗ ○ ○ ○ ○ ○ ○	_____	_____	_____
9.	⊗ ⊗ ⊗ ⊗ ⊗ ○ ○ ○	_____	_____	_____
10.	⊗ ⊗ ⊗ ○ ○	_____	_____	_____

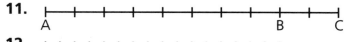

From A to B is what fractional part of the distance from A to C?

11. $\frac{8}{10}$ or $\frac{4}{5}$

12. _____

13. _____

14. _____

15. _____

16. _____

17. _____

18. _____

19. _____

20. _____

Fractional Parts

Name the fractional part of each figure that is shaded.

1. $\frac{5}{8}$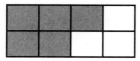

2. _____

3. _____

4. _____

5. _____

6. _____

7. _____

8. _____

9. _____

10. _____

Complete each of the following.

11. Five cents is $\frac{1}{20}$ of a dollar.

12. Seventy-five cents is _____ of a dollar.

13. Twenty cents is _____ of a dollar.

14. _____ cents is $\frac{1}{10}$ of a dollar.

15. _____ cents is $\frac{1}{4}$ of a dollar.

16. _____ dollars is $\frac{3}{5}$ of five dollars.

Basic Computation Series 2000: Understanding Fractions
SECTION 1 Common Fractions, Equivalent Fractions, and Ratio and Proportion

15

NAME _____ DATE _____

Equivalent Fractions

Write five fractions equivalent to the given fraction.

1. $\frac{1}{2}$ $\frac{2}{4}$ $\frac{3}{6}$ $\frac{4}{8}$ $\frac{5}{10}$ $\frac{6}{12}$

2. $\frac{1}{3}$ _____   _____   _____   _____   _____

3. $\frac{2}{3}$ _____   _____   _____   _____   _____

4. $\frac{1}{4}$ _____   _____   _____   _____   _____

5. $\frac{3}{4}$ _____   _____   _____   _____   _____

6. $\frac{1}{5}$ _____   _____   _____   _____   _____

7. $\frac{2}{5}$ _____   _____   _____   _____   _____

8. $\frac{3}{5}$ _____   _____   _____   _____   _____

9. $\frac{4}{5}$ _____   _____   _____   _____   _____

10. $\frac{1}{6}$ _____   _____   _____   _____   _____

Fill in the blanks to make equivalent fractions.

11. $\frac{1}{2} = \frac{2}{4}$

12. $\frac{2}{3} = \frac{}{6}$

13. $\frac{1}{4} = \frac{}{12}$

14. $\frac{1}{5} = \frac{}{25}$

15. $\frac{2}{5} = \frac{}{15}$

16. $\frac{3}{4} = \frac{}{16}$

17. $\frac{1}{2} = \frac{}{10}$

18. $\frac{1}{4} = \frac{}{20}$

19. $\frac{1}{3} = \frac{}{12}$

20. $\frac{3}{5} = \frac{}{20}$

21. $\frac{1}{5} = \frac{}{15}$

22. $\frac{1}{3} = \frac{}{9}$

23. $\frac{3}{4} = \frac{}{20}$

24. $\frac{2}{3} = \frac{}{12}$

25. $\frac{1}{4} = \frac{}{8}$

26. $\frac{1}{4} = \frac{}{16}$

27. $\frac{1}{5} = \frac{}{20}$

28. $\frac{1}{2} = \frac{}{16}$

29. $\frac{3}{5} = \frac{}{15}$

30. $\frac{1}{6} = \frac{}{18}$

Reducing Fractions

Rewrite each fraction in lowest terms.

1. $\frac{4}{12} = \underline{\quad \frac{1}{3} \quad}$

2. $\frac{8}{12} = \underline{\qquad}$

3. $\frac{3}{18} = \underline{\qquad}$

4. $\frac{10}{15} = \underline{\qquad}$

5. $\frac{4}{8} = \underline{\qquad}$

6. $\frac{12}{16} = \underline{\qquad}$

7. $\frac{5}{25} = \underline{\qquad}$

8. $\frac{4}{16} = \underline{\qquad}$

9. $\frac{5}{35} = \underline{\qquad}$

10. $\frac{10}{20} = \underline{\qquad}$

11. $\frac{4}{6} = \underline{\qquad}$

12. $\frac{6}{10} = \underline{\qquad}$

13. $\frac{8}{10} = \underline{\qquad}$

14. $\frac{4}{20} = \underline{\qquad}$

15. $\frac{12}{18} = \underline{\qquad}$

16. $\frac{3}{24} = \underline{\qquad}$

17. $\frac{7}{35} = \underline{\qquad}$

18. $\frac{6}{24} = \underline{\qquad}$

19. $\frac{14}{32} = \underline{\qquad}$

20. $\frac{7}{28} = \underline{\qquad}$

Basic Computation Series 2000: Understanding Fractions
SECTION 1 Common Fractions, Equivalent Fractions, and Ratio and Proportion

17

Equivalent Fractions

Write five fractions equivalent to the given fraction.

1. $\frac{3}{4}$ $\frac{6}{8}$ $\frac{9}{12}$ $\frac{12}{16}$ $\frac{15}{20}$ $\frac{18}{24}$

2. $\frac{2}{5}$ _____   _____   _____   _____   _____

3. $\frac{5}{6}$ _____   _____   _____   _____   _____

4. $\frac{3}{7}$ _____   _____   _____   _____   _____

5. $\frac{3}{8}$ _____   _____   _____   _____   _____

6. $\frac{1}{3}$ _____   _____   _____   _____   _____

7. $\frac{5}{8}$ _____   _____   _____   _____   _____

8. $\frac{7}{9}$ _____   _____   _____   _____   _____

9. $\frac{3}{5}$ _____   _____   _____   _____   _____

10. $\frac{8}{9}$ _____   _____   _____   _____   _____

Fill in the blanks to make equivalent fractions.

11. $\frac{1}{2} = \frac{5}{10}$

12. $\frac{2}{3} = \frac{}{15}$

13. $\frac{1}{4} = \frac{}{20}$

14. $\frac{1}{5} = \frac{}{50}$

15. $\frac{2}{5} = \frac{}{35}$

16. $\frac{3}{4} = \frac{}{12}$

17. $\frac{1}{2} = \frac{}{20}$

18. $\frac{1}{8} = \frac{}{16}$

19. $\frac{1}{3} = \frac{}{24}$

20. $\frac{3}{5} = \frac{}{45}$

21. $\frac{1}{5} = \frac{}{20}$

22. $\frac{1}{3} = \frac{}{18}$

23. $\frac{3}{4} = \frac{}{40}$

24. $\frac{2}{3} = \frac{}{18}$

25. $\frac{2}{7} = \frac{}{28}$

26. $\frac{3}{4} = \frac{}{20}$

27. $\frac{1}{5} = \frac{}{25}$

28. $\frac{2}{7} = \frac{}{21}$

29. $\frac{3}{5} = \frac{}{30}$

30. $\frac{1}{6} = \frac{}{36}$

18

Basic Computation Series 2000: Understanding Fractions
SECTION 1 Common Fractions, Equivalent Fractions, and Ratio and Proportion

Reducing Fractions

Rewrite each fraction in lowest terms.

1. $\frac{15}{30} = \underline{\quad \frac{1}{2} \quad}$

2. $\frac{20}{30} = \underline{\qquad}$

3. $\frac{10}{15} = \underline{\qquad}$

4. $\frac{15}{25} = \underline{\qquad}$

5. $\frac{16}{64} = \underline{\qquad}$

6. $\frac{36}{42} = \underline{\qquad}$

7. $\frac{10}{30} = \underline{\qquad}$

8. $\frac{35}{42} = \underline{\qquad}$

9. $\frac{42}{60} = \underline{\qquad}$

10. $\frac{26}{39} = \underline{\qquad}$

11. $\frac{10}{18} = \underline{\qquad}$

12. $\frac{16}{24} = \underline{\qquad}$

13. $\frac{16}{28} = \underline{\qquad}$

14. $\frac{35}{49} = \underline{\qquad}$

15. $\frac{18}{30} = \underline{\qquad}$

16. $\frac{18}{20} = \underline{\qquad}$

17. $\frac{9}{15} = \underline{\qquad}$

18. $\frac{6}{18} = \underline{\qquad}$

19. $\frac{14}{24} = \underline{\qquad}$

20. $\frac{42}{48} = \underline{\qquad}$

Basic Computation Series 2000: Understanding Fractions
SECTION 1 Common Fractions, Equivalent Fractions, and Ratio and Proportion

19

NAME _____   DATE _____

Equivalent Fractions

Write five fractions equivalent to the given fraction.

1. $\frac{5}{7}$ $\frac{10}{14}$ $\frac{15}{21}$ $\frac{20}{28}$ $\frac{25}{35}$ $\frac{30}{42}$

2. $\frac{1}{2}$ _____   _____   _____   _____   _____

3. $\frac{3}{5}$ _____   _____   _____   _____   _____

4. $\frac{6}{7}$ _____   _____   _____   _____   _____

5. $\frac{7}{10}$ _____   _____   _____   _____   _____

6. $\frac{4}{9}$ _____   _____   _____   _____   _____

7. $\frac{1}{4}$ _____   _____   _____   _____   _____

8. $\frac{6}{11}$ _____   _____   _____   _____   _____

9. $\frac{4}{5}$ _____   _____   _____   _____   _____

10. $\frac{5}{13}$ _____   _____   _____   _____   _____

Fill in the blanks to make equivalent fractions.

11. $\frac{1}{2} = \frac{15}{30}$ 21. $\frac{1}{5} = \frac{}{35}$

12. $\frac{2}{3} = \frac{}{21}$ 22. $\frac{7}{8} = \frac{}{48}$

13. $\frac{1}{4} = \frac{}{44}$ 23. $\frac{3}{4} = \frac{}{24}$

14. $\frac{2}{5} = \frac{}{30}$ 24. $\frac{6}{7} = \frac{}{42}$

15. $\frac{5}{9} = \frac{}{36}$ 25. $\frac{7}{10} = \frac{}{40}$

16. $\frac{3}{4} = \frac{}{32}$ 26. $\frac{1}{4} = \frac{}{36}$

17. $\frac{4}{5} = \frac{}{40}$ 27. $\frac{7}{12} = \frac{}{48}$

18. $\frac{9}{10} = \frac{}{20}$ 28. $\frac{5}{11} = \frac{}{55}$

19. $\frac{1}{3} = \frac{}{27}$ 29. $\frac{11}{12} = \frac{}{72}$

20. $\frac{3}{5} = \frac{}{40}$ 30. $\frac{1}{6} = \frac{}{60}$

Basic Computation Series 2000: Understanding Fractions
SECTION 1 Common Fractions, Equivalent Fractions, and Ratio and Proportion

NAME   DATE

Reducing Fractions

Rewrite each fraction in lowest terms.

1. $\frac{25}{35} = \frac{5}{7}$	**11.** $\frac{16}{28} = $ _____
2. $\frac{16}{32} = $ _____	**12.** $\frac{15}{35} = $ _____
3. $\frac{12}{36} = $ _____	**13.** $\frac{14}{35} = $ _____
4. $\frac{21}{49} = $ _____	**14.** $\frac{48}{64} = $ _____
5. $\frac{12}{144} = $ _____	**15.** $\frac{40}{100} = $ _____
6. $\frac{15}{30} = $ _____	**16.** $\frac{27}{36} = $ _____
7. $\frac{45}{50} = $ _____	**17.** $\frac{26}{30} = $ _____
8. $\frac{28}{35} = $ _____	**18.** $\frac{15}{36} = $ _____
9. $\frac{45}{90} = $ _____	**19.** $\frac{90}{108} = $ _____
10. $\frac{70}{150} = $ _____	**20.** $\frac{27}{72} = $ _____

Copyright © Dale Seymour Publications®

Equivalent Fractions

Write five fractions equivalent to the given fraction.

1. $\frac{1}{5}$ $\frac{2}{10}$ $\frac{3}{15}$ $\frac{4}{20}$ $\frac{5}{25}$ $\frac{6}{30}$

2. $\frac{4}{7}$ _____   _____   _____   _____   _____

3. $\frac{2}{3}$ _____   _____   _____   _____   _____

4. $\frac{7}{8}$ _____   _____   _____   _____   _____

5. $\frac{1}{12}$ _____   _____   _____   _____   _____

6. $\frac{2}{5}$ _____   _____   _____   _____   _____

7. $\frac{5}{9}$ _____   _____   _____   _____   _____

8. $\frac{5}{8}$ _____   _____   _____   _____   _____

9. $\frac{8}{13}$ _____   _____   _____   _____   _____

10. $\frac{3}{4}$ _____   _____   _____   _____   _____

Fill in the blanks to make equivalent fractions.

11. $\frac{1}{12} = \frac{3}{36}$ **21.** $\frac{1}{5} = \frac{}{45}$

12. $\frac{2}{3} = \frac{}{42}$ **22.** $\frac{3}{8} = \frac{}{40}$

13. $\frac{1}{4} = \frac{}{56}$ **23.** $\frac{5}{7} = \frac{}{56}$

14. $\frac{1}{5} = \frac{}{55}$ **24.** $\frac{9}{11} = \frac{}{77}$

15. $\frac{7}{16} = \frac{}{64}$ **25.** $\frac{5}{12} = \frac{}{84}$

16. $\frac{3}{14} = \frac{}{42}$ **26.** $\frac{4}{7} = \frac{}{35}$

17. $\frac{1}{2} = \frac{}{50}$ **27.** $\frac{7}{15} = \frac{}{45}$

18. $\frac{7}{12} = \frac{}{60}$ **28.** $\frac{8}{9} = \frac{}{63}$

19. $\frac{3}{5} = \frac{}{40}$ **29.** $\frac{15}{16} = \frac{}{64}$

20. $\frac{7}{8} = \frac{}{48}$ **30.** $\frac{9}{25} = \frac{}{75}$

Basic Computation Series 2000: Understanding Fractions
SECTION 1 Common Fractions, Equivalent Fractions, and Ratio and Proportion

Reducing Fractions

Rewrite each fraction in lowest terms.

1. $\frac{40}{50} =$ ___ $\frac{4}{5}$ ___

2. $\frac{21}{24} =$ _____

3. $\frac{18}{36} =$ _____

4. $\frac{20}{30} =$ _____

5. $\frac{11}{22} =$ _____

6. $\frac{34}{36} =$ _____

7. $\frac{16}{20} =$ _____

8. $\frac{18}{42} =$ _____

9. $\frac{63}{84} =$ _____

10. $\frac{75}{80} =$ _____

11. $\frac{14}{28} =$ _____

12. $\frac{16}{32} =$ _____

13. $\frac{24}{36} =$ _____

14. $\frac{24}{144} =$ _____

15. $\frac{24}{256} =$ _____

16. $\frac{45}{50} =$ _____

17. $\frac{27}{30} =$ _____

18. $\frac{16}{40} =$ _____

19. $\frac{35}{56} =$ _____

20. $\frac{189}{210} =$ _____

Basic Computation Series 2000: Understanding Fractions
SECTION 1 Common Fractions, Equivalent Fractions, and Ratio and Proportion

23

Equivalent Fractions

Write five fractions equivalent to the given fraction.

1. $\frac{3}{4}$ $\frac{6}{8}$ $\frac{9}{12}$ $\frac{12}{16}$ $\frac{15}{20}$ $\frac{18}{24}$

2. $\frac{4}{5}$ _____   _____   _____   _____   _____

3. $\frac{6}{7}$ _____   _____   _____   _____   _____

4. $\frac{5}{6}$ _____   _____   _____   _____   _____

5. $\frac{5}{12}$ _____   _____   _____   _____   _____

6. $\frac{5}{8}$ _____   _____   _____   _____   _____

7. $\frac{2}{3}$ _____   _____   _____   _____   _____

8. $\frac{5}{9}$ _____   _____   _____   _____   _____

9. $\frac{1}{2}$ _____   _____   _____   _____   _____

10. $\frac{3}{8}$ _____   _____   _____   _____   _____

Fill in the blanks to make equivalent fractions.

11. $\frac{1}{2} = \frac{5}{10}$

12. $\frac{4}{5} = \frac{}{15}$

13. $\frac{9}{10} = \frac{}{50}$

14. $\frac{6}{7} = \frac{}{28}$

15. $\frac{3}{8} = \frac{}{40}$

16. $\frac{5}{8} = \frac{}{32}$

17. $\frac{7}{16} = \frac{}{64}$

18. $\frac{2}{7} = \frac{}{63}$

19. $\frac{3}{4} = \frac{}{16}$

20. $\frac{5}{11} = \frac{}{77}$

21. $\frac{7}{9} = \frac{}{27}$

22. $\frac{5}{12} = \frac{}{36}$

23. $\frac{7}{11} = \frac{}{33}$

24. $\frac{16}{17} = \frac{}{34}$

25. $\frac{9}{13} = \frac{}{39}$

26. $\frac{3}{4} = \frac{}{24}$

27. $\frac{4}{7} = \frac{}{28}$

28. $\frac{5}{13} = \frac{}{52}$

29. $\frac{4}{9} = \frac{}{45}$

30. $\frac{6}{7} = \frac{}{35}$

Reducing Fractions

Rewrite each fraction in lowest terms.

1. $\frac{16}{24}$ = $\frac{2}{3}$

2. $\frac{20}{35}$ = _____

3. $\frac{20}{36}$ = _____

4. $\frac{20}{30}$ = _____

5. $\frac{45}{50}$ = _____

6. $\frac{40}{45}$ = _____

7. $\frac{15}{45}$ = _____

8. $\frac{26}{39}$ = _____

9. $\frac{21}{49}$ = _____

10. $\frac{10}{18}$ = _____

11. $\frac{20}{25}$ = _____

12. $\frac{18}{45}$ = _____

13. $\frac{25}{45}$ = _____

14. $\frac{14}{35}$ = _____

15. $\frac{9}{15}$ = _____

16. $\frac{32}{40}$ = _____

17. $\frac{30}{40}$ = _____

18. $\frac{15}{25}$ = _____

19. $\frac{16}{28}$ = _____

20. $\frac{4}{20}$ = _____

Basic Computation Series 2000: Understanding Fractions
SECTION 1 Common Fractions, Equivalent Fractions, and Ratio and Proportion

25

Equivalent Fractions

Fill in the blanks to make equivalent fractions.

1. $\frac{1}{3} = \frac{2}{6}$	**11.** $\frac{5}{6} = \frac{}{78}$	**21.** $\frac{3}{4} = \frac{}{36}$
2. $\frac{1}{4} = \frac{}{8}$	**12.** $\frac{4}{9} = \frac{}{99}$	**22.** $\frac{1}{8} = \frac{}{80}$
3. $\frac{2}{3} = \frac{}{12}$	**13.** $\frac{1}{5} = \frac{}{125}$	**23.** $\frac{1}{4} = \frac{}{44}$
4. $\frac{1}{9} = \frac{}{36}$	**14.** $\frac{2}{3} = \frac{}{27}$	**24.** $\frac{3}{7} = \frac{}{21}$
5. $\frac{2}{7} = \frac{}{21}$	**15.** $\frac{7}{9} = \frac{}{63}$	**25.** $\frac{1}{2} = \frac{}{16}$
6. $\frac{6}{7} = \frac{}{42}$	**16.** $\frac{1}{7} = \frac{}{49}$	**26.** $\frac{3}{5} = \frac{}{25}$
7. $\frac{7}{9} = \frac{}{54}$	**17.** $\frac{1}{2} = \frac{}{24}$	**27.** $\frac{3}{8} = \frac{}{48}$
8. $\frac{3}{8} = \frac{}{72}$	**18.** $\frac{3}{4} = \frac{}{12}$	**28.** $\frac{3}{7} = \frac{}{91}$
9. $\frac{5}{6} = \frac{}{42}$	**19.** $\frac{4}{7} = \frac{}{21}$	**29.** $\frac{5}{9} = \frac{}{117}$
10. $\frac{1}{5} = \frac{}{40}$	**20.** $\frac{5}{6} = \frac{}{54}$	**30.** $\frac{1}{5} = \frac{}{60}$

26

Basic Computation Series 2000: Understanding Fractions
SECTION 1 Common Fractions, Equivalent Fractions, and Ratio and Proportion

Reducing Fractions

Rewrite each fraction in lowest terms.

1. $\frac{4}{8} =$ _____ $\frac{1}{2}$ _____   **11.** $\frac{15}{90} =$ _____   **21.** $\frac{18}{27} =$ _____

2. $\frac{10}{30} =$ _____   **12.** $\frac{16}{36} =$ _____   **22.** $\frac{15}{25} =$ _____

3. $\frac{3}{12} =$ _____   **13.** $\frac{12}{15} =$ _____   **23.** $\frac{12}{18} =$ _____

4. $\frac{3}{6} =$ _____   **14.** $\frac{18}{30} =$ _____   **24.** $\frac{27}{45} =$ _____

5. $\frac{15}{45} =$ _____   **15.** $\frac{14}{21} =$ _____   **25.** $\frac{26}{39} =$ _____

6. $\frac{3}{27} =$ _____   **16.** $\frac{75}{120} =$ _____   **26.** $\frac{15}{35} =$ _____

7. $\frac{8}{20} =$ _____   **17.** $\frac{54}{60} =$ _____   **27.** $\frac{34}{51} =$ _____

8. $\frac{4}{6} =$ _____   **18.** $\frac{20}{40} =$ _____   **28.** $\frac{5}{10} =$ _____

9. $\frac{8}{10} =$ _____   **19.** $\frac{20}{50} =$ _____   **29.** $\frac{15}{40} =$ _____

10. $\frac{4}{20} =$ _____   **20.** $\frac{12}{28} =$ _____   **30.** $\frac{60}{96} =$ _____

Basic Computation Series 2000: Understanding Fractions
SECTION 1 Common Fractions, Equivalent Fractions, and Ratio and Proportion

27

Equivalent Fractions

Fill in the blanks to make equivalent fractions.

1. $\frac{1}{2} = \frac{2}{4}$

2. $\frac{5}{11} = \frac{}{44}$

3. $\frac{2}{3} = \frac{}{24}$

4. $\frac{3}{8} = \frac{}{24}$

5. $\frac{2}{3} = \frac{}{15}$

6. $\frac{5}{9} = \frac{}{72}$

7. $\frac{1}{8} = \frac{}{16}$

8. $\frac{3}{4} = \frac{}{20}$

9. $\frac{2}{5} = \frac{}{80}$

10. $\frac{7}{11} = \frac{}{44}$

11. $\frac{3}{4} = \frac{}{36}$

12. $\frac{5}{6} = \frac{}{78}$

13. $\frac{3}{8} = \frac{}{32}$

14. $\frac{5}{6} = \frac{}{18}$

15. $\frac{2}{7} = \frac{}{42}$

16. $\frac{3}{5} = \frac{}{15}$

17. $\frac{5}{8} = \frac{}{56}$

18. $\frac{2}{3} = \frac{}{36}$

19. $\frac{2}{3} = \frac{}{30}$

20. $\frac{3}{5} = \frac{}{25}$

21. $\frac{4}{7} = \frac{}{56}$

22. $\frac{2}{5} = \frac{}{70}$

23. $\frac{2}{7} = \frac{}{35}$

24. $\frac{4}{7} = \frac{}{49}$

25. $\frac{5}{9} = \frac{}{81}$

26. $\frac{5}{8} = \frac{}{48}$

27. $\frac{5}{6} = \frac{}{42}$

28. $\frac{5}{6} = \frac{}{48}$

29. $\frac{3}{13} = \frac{}{78}$

30. $\frac{1}{3} = \frac{}{42}$

28

Basic Computation Series 2000: Understanding Fractions
SECTION 1 Common Fractions, Equivalent Fractions, and Ratio and Proportion

Reducing Fractions

Rewrite each fraction in lowest terms.

1. $\frac{15}{18}$ = $\frac{5}{6}$	**11.** $\frac{10}{35}$ = _____	**21.** $\frac{27}{33}$ = _____
2. $\frac{21}{35}$ = _____	**12.** $\frac{60}{84}$ = _____	**22.** $\frac{12}{20}$ = _____
3. $\frac{17}{51}$ = _____	**13.** $\frac{24}{27}$ = _____	**23.** $\frac{30}{36}$ = _____
4. $\frac{6}{9}$ = _____	**14.** $\frac{16}{28}$ = _____	**24.** $\frac{24}{64}$ = _____
5. $\frac{4}{20}$ = _____	**15.** $\frac{18}{54}$ = _____	**25.** $\frac{28}{42}$ = _____
6. $\frac{44}{77}$ = _____	**16.** $\frac{9}{18}$ = _____	**26.** $\frac{29}{58}$ = _____
7. $\frac{12}{32}$ = _____	**17.** $\frac{24}{56}$ = _____	**27.** $\frac{34}{51}$ = _____
8. $\frac{32}{40}$ = _____	**18.** $\frac{5}{40}$ = _____	**28.** $\frac{10}{60}$ = _____
9. $\frac{20}{44}$ = _____	**19.** $\frac{13}{52}$ = _____	**29.** $\frac{27}{36}$ = _____
10. $\frac{20}{30}$ = _____	**20.** $\frac{25}{35}$ = _____	**30.** $\frac{48}{60}$ = _____

Basic Computation Series 2000: Understanding Fractions
SECTION 1 Common Fractions, Equivalent Fractions, and Ratio and Proportion

Equivalent Fractions

Fill in the blanks to make equivalent fractions.

1. $\frac{7}{20} = \frac{14}{40}$	**11.** $\frac{1}{6} = \frac{}{18}$	**21.** $\frac{4}{25} = \frac{}{75}$
2. $\frac{5}{8} = \frac{}{24}$	**12.** $\frac{4}{7} = \frac{}{35}$	**22.** $\frac{5}{6} = \frac{}{12}$
3. $\frac{3}{8} = \frac{}{40}$	**13.** $\frac{5}{16} = \frac{}{80}$	**23.** $\frac{5}{9} = \frac{}{36}$
4. $\frac{3}{4} = \frac{}{16}$	**14.** $\frac{3}{10} = \frac{}{30}$	**24.** $\frac{3}{5} = \frac{}{30}$
5. $\frac{2}{5} = \frac{}{10}$	**15.** $\frac{11}{18} = \frac{}{36}$	**25.** $\frac{5}{6} = \frac{}{42}$
6. $\frac{3}{4} = \frac{}{20}$	**16.** $\frac{4}{5} = \frac{}{20}$	**26.** $\frac{7}{20} = \frac{}{60}$
7. $\frac{7}{12} = \frac{}{24}$	**17.** $\frac{5}{7} = \frac{}{42}$	**27.** $\frac{13}{36} = \frac{}{108}$
8. $\frac{5}{14} = \frac{}{28}$	**18.** $\frac{3}{10} = \frac{}{100}$	**28.** $\frac{2}{9} = \frac{}{18}$
9. $\frac{9}{10} = \frac{}{80}$	**19.** $\frac{5}{12} = \frac{}{36}$	**29.** $\frac{3}{4} = \frac{}{32}$
10. $\frac{3}{7} = \frac{}{21}$	**20.** $\frac{7}{15} = \frac{}{45}$	**30.** $\frac{7}{9} = \frac{}{45}$

30

Basic Computation Series 2000: Understanding Fractions
SECTION 1 Common Fractions, Equivalent Fractions, and Ratio and Proportion

Reducing Fractions

Rewrite each fraction in lowest terms.

1. $\frac{34}{51}$ = $\frac{2}{3}$	**11.** $\frac{72}{84}$ = _____	**21.** $\frac{70}{84}$ = _____
2. $\frac{60}{72}$ = _____	**12.** $\frac{18}{24}$ = _____	**22.** $\frac{22}{77}$ = _____
3. $\frac{16}{60}$ = _____	**13.** $\frac{45}{63}$ = _____	**23.** $\frac{28}{35}$ = _____
4. $\frac{18}{42}$ = _____	**14.** $\frac{38}{57}$ = _____	**24.** $\frac{22}{99}$ = _____
5. $\frac{16}{28}$ = _____	**15.** $\frac{45}{54}$ = _____	**25.** $\frac{33}{39}$ = _____
6. $\frac{40}{56}$ = _____	**16.** $\frac{18}{45}$ = _____	**26.** $\frac{56}{80}$ = _____
7. $\frac{40}{64}$ = _____	**17.** $\frac{9}{36}$ = _____	**27.** $\frac{42}{63}$ = _____
8. $\frac{45}{72}$ = _____	**18.** $\frac{12}{144}$ = _____	**28.** $\frac{7}{56}$ = _____
9. $\frac{42}{70}$ = _____	**19.** $\frac{26}{39}$ = _____	**29.** $\frac{10}{45}$ = _____
10. $\frac{6}{18}$ = _____	**20.** $\frac{28}{49}$ = _____	**30.** $\frac{15}{27}$ = _____

Basic Computation Series 2000: Understanding Fractions
SECTION 1 Common Fractions, Equivalent Fractions, and Ratio and Proportion

31

Equivalent Fractions

Fill in the blanks to make equivalent fractions.

1. $\frac{3}{4} = \frac{15}{20}$	**11.** $\frac{4}{9} = \frac{}{36}$	**21.** $\frac{3}{4} = \frac{}{12}$
2. $\frac{4}{5} = \frac{}{30}$	**12.** $\frac{6}{7} = \frac{}{42}$	**22.** $\frac{2}{3} = \frac{}{12}$
3. $\frac{9}{14} = \frac{}{42}$	**13.** $\frac{3}{13} = \frac{}{78}$	**23.** $\frac{3}{7} = \frac{}{35}$
4. $\frac{5}{6} = \frac{}{36}$	**14.** $\frac{7}{8} = \frac{}{72}$	**24.** $\frac{8}{9} = \frac{}{36}$
5. $\frac{2}{7} = \frac{}{21}$	**15.** $\frac{5}{12} = \frac{}{60}$	**25.** $\frac{3}{4} = \frac{}{28}$
6. $\frac{3}{4} = \frac{}{16}$	**16.** $\frac{4}{7} = \frac{}{28}$	**26.** $\frac{7}{15} = \frac{}{75}$
7. $\frac{5}{8} = \frac{}{32}$	**17.** $\frac{5}{8} = \frac{}{24}$	**27.** $\frac{4}{15} = \frac{}{30}$
8. $\frac{3}{4} = \frac{}{44}$	**18.** $\frac{5}{12} = \frac{}{36}$	**28.** $\frac{4}{9} = \frac{}{18}$
9. $\frac{5}{9} = \frac{}{45}$	**19.** $\frac{1}{3} = \frac{}{42}$	**29.** $\frac{2}{3} = \frac{}{15}$
10. $\frac{2}{9} = \frac{}{18}$	**20.** $\frac{3}{16} = \frac{}{80}$	**30.** $\frac{5}{7} = \frac{}{14}$

32

Basic Computation Series 2000: Understanding Fractions
SECTION 1 Common Fractions, Equivalent Fractions, and Ratio and Proportion

Reducing Fractions

Rewrite each fraction in lowest terms.

1. $\frac{8}{18} =$ $\frac{4}{9}$	**11.** $\frac{18}{30} =$ _____	**21.** $\frac{46}{64} =$ _____
2. $\frac{32}{48} =$ _____	**12.** $\frac{8}{28} =$ _____	**22.** $\frac{3}{18} =$ _____
3. $\frac{31}{62} =$ _____	**13.** $\frac{6}{18} =$ _____	**23.** $\frac{16}{24} =$ _____
4. $\frac{20}{50} =$ _____	**14.** $\frac{21}{49} =$ _____	**24.** $\frac{40}{64} =$ _____
5. $\frac{50}{70} =$ _____	**15.** $\frac{14}{32} =$ _____	**25.** $\frac{10}{24} =$ _____
6. $\frac{12}{48} =$ _____	**16.** $\frac{12}{24} =$ _____	**26.** $\frac{22}{55} =$ _____
7. $\frac{6}{12} =$ _____	**17.** $\frac{14}{24} =$ _____	**27.** $\frac{102}{106} =$ _____
8. $\frac{33}{57} =$ _____	**18.** $\frac{11}{88} =$ _____	**28.** $\frac{48}{56} =$ _____
9. $\frac{41}{82} =$ _____	**19.** $\frac{10}{50} =$ _____	**29.** $\frac{40}{48} =$ _____
10. $\frac{48}{84} =$ _____	**20.** $\frac{35}{75} =$ _____	**30.** $\frac{24}{108} =$ _____

Basic Computation Series 2000: Understanding Fractions
SECTION 1 Common Fractions, Equivalent Fractions, and Ratio and Proportion

Equivalent Fractions

Fill in the blanks to make equivalent fractions.

1. $\frac{1}{2} = \frac{4}{8}$

2. $\frac{6}{11} = \frac{}{55}$

3. $\frac{6}{21} = \frac{}{126}$

4. $\frac{3}{5} = \frac{}{55}$

5. $\frac{8}{13} = \frac{}{39}$

6. $\frac{3}{4} = \frac{}{24}$

7. $\frac{1}{3} = \frac{}{9}$

8. $\frac{5}{9} = \frac{}{18}$

9. $\frac{7}{25} = \frac{}{125}$

10. $\frac{9}{13} = \frac{}{26}$

11. $\frac{7}{16} = \frac{}{48}$

12. $\frac{5}{9} = \frac{}{54}$

13. $\frac{3}{4} = \frac{}{28}$

14. $\frac{8}{13} = \frac{}{26}$

15. $\frac{2}{3} = \frac{}{24}$

16. $\frac{6}{11} = \frac{}{77}$

17. $\frac{9}{11} = \frac{}{55}$

18. $\frac{6}{7} = \frac{}{42}$

19. $\frac{4}{5} = \frac{}{35}$

20. $\frac{5}{12} = \frac{}{60}$

21. $\frac{5}{6} = \frac{}{30}$

22. $\frac{9}{16} = \frac{}{32}$

23. $\frac{16}{21} = \frac{}{42}$

24. $\frac{1}{2} = \frac{}{50}$

25. $\frac{5}{6} = \frac{}{42}$

26. $\frac{7}{8} = \frac{}{24}$

27. $\frac{11}{12} = \frac{}{60}$

28. $\frac{8}{25} = \frac{}{50}$

29. $\frac{8}{27} = \frac{}{54}$

30. $\frac{7}{13} = \frac{}{52}$

34

Basic Computation Series 2000: Understanding Fractions
SECTION 1 Common Fractions, Equivalent Fractions, and Ratio and Proportion

Reducing Fractions

Rewrite each fraction in lowest terms.

1. $\frac{2}{4}$ = $\frac{1}{2}$

2. $\frac{26}{65}$ = _____

3. $\frac{9}{54}$ = _____

4. $\frac{18}{21}$ = _____

5. $\frac{9}{81}$ = _____

6. $\frac{4}{16}$ = _____

7. $\frac{7}{21}$ = _____

8. $\frac{21}{27}$ = _____

9. $\frac{12}{27}$ = _____

10. $\frac{33}{55}$ = _____

11. $\frac{22}{33}$ = _____

12. $\frac{6}{36}$ = _____

13. $\frac{9}{57}$ = _____

14. $\frac{10}{15}$ = _____

15. $\frac{28}{52}$ = _____

16. $\frac{14}{49}$ = _____

17. $\frac{12}{30}$ = _____

18. $\frac{13}{91}$ = _____

19. $\frac{12}{14}$ = _____

20. $\frac{20}{36}$ = _____

21. $\frac{24}{32}$ = _____

22. $\frac{30}{70}$ = _____

23. $\frac{32}{40}$ = _____

24. $\frac{24}{42}$ = _____

25. $\frac{2}{6}$ = _____

26. $\frac{30}{75}$ = _____

27. $\frac{18}{45}$ = _____

28. $\frac{12}{54}$ = _____

29. $\frac{63}{81}$ = _____

30. $\frac{50}{80}$ = _____

Basic Computation Series 2000: Understanding Fractions
SECTION 1 Common Fractions, Equivalent Fractions, and Ratio and Proportion

35

Proportions

Use cross products to replace the ? with = or ≠ to make a true statement.

1. $\frac{5}{9}$? $\frac{20}{36}$

7. $\frac{1}{2}$? $\frac{23}{86}$

2. $\frac{3}{7}$? $\frac{21}{49}$

8. $\frac{4}{5}$? $\frac{28}{35}$

3. $\frac{2}{3}$? $\frac{16}{27}$

9. $\frac{2}{3}$? $\frac{17}{18}$

4. $\frac{3}{5}$? $\frac{21}{25}$

10. $\frac{22}{24}$? $\frac{33}{36}$

5. $\frac{7}{8}$? $\frac{28}{35}$

11. $\frac{7}{18}$? $\frac{4}{9}$

6. $\frac{3}{4}$? $\frac{16}{12}$

12. $\frac{17}{25}$? $\frac{34}{60}$

Complete each of the following by replacing the ? in each statement to make a proportion.

13. $\frac{?}{15} = \frac{3}{5}$

19. $\frac{?}{42} = \frac{1}{2}$

14. $\frac{?}{95} = \frac{4}{190}$

20. $\frac{?}{9} = \frac{35}{63}$

15. $\frac{?}{60} = \frac{6}{10}$

21. $\frac{7}{9} = \frac{?}{36}$

16. $\frac{?}{32} = \frac{7}{16}$

22. $\frac{8}{15} = \frac{?}{45}$

17. $\frac{4}{?} = \frac{12}{60}$

23. $\frac{7}{23} = \frac{42}{?}$

18. $\frac{?}{16} = \frac{12}{32}$

24. $\frac{2}{15} = \frac{20}{?}$

36

Basic Computation Series 2000: Understanding Fractions
SECTION 1 Common Fractions, Equivalent Fractions, and Ratio and Proportion

Ratio and Proportion Word Problems

Solve each problem using a proportion.

1. A cyclist travels 225 kilometers in 7 hours. Traveling at the same rate, how far will he travel in 35 hours?

2. If a yardstick (3 feet long) casts a shadow 15 centimeters long at the same time a nearby tree casts a shadow 150 centimeters long, how tall is the tree in feet?

3. If the ratio of Bob's salary to his father's salary is 2 to 7, and Bob makes $216 in a month, how much does his father make?

4. The ratio of the area of Domingo's house to that of Pedro's house is $\frac{3}{5}$. If Pedro's house has an area of 2,250 square feet, what is the area of Domingo's house?

Basic Computation Series 2000: Understanding Fractions
SECTION 1   Common Fractions, Equivalent Fractions, and Ratio and Proportion

37

Proportions

Use cross products to replace the ? with = or ≠ to make a true statement.

1. $\frac{7}{10}$? $\frac{14}{24}$

2. $\frac{1}{4}$? $\frac{7}{32}$

3. $\frac{1}{6}$? $\frac{16}{96}$

4. $\frac{2}{5}$? $\frac{30}{75}$

5. $\frac{2}{3}$? $\frac{14}{24}$

6. $\frac{4}{5}$? $\frac{16}{20}$

7. $\frac{9}{10}$? $\frac{18}{20}$

8. $\frac{1}{7}$? $\frac{5}{28}$

9. $\frac{8}{25}$? $\frac{21}{40}$

10. $\frac{5}{16}$? $\frac{8}{12}$

11. $\frac{4}{21}$? $\frac{8}{42}$

12. $\frac{15}{23}$? $\frac{30}{46}$

Complete each of the following by replacing the ? in each statement to make a proportion.

13. $\frac{?}{84} = \frac{4}{28}$

14. $\frac{?}{52} = \frac{5}{13}$

15. $\frac{55}{?} = \frac{5}{17}$

16. $\frac{72}{?} = \frac{6}{13}$

17. $\frac{?}{78} = \frac{3}{39}$

18. $\frac{36}{?} = \frac{18}{23}$

19. $\frac{24}{?} = \frac{8}{23}$

20. $\frac{?}{56} = \frac{13}{28}$

21. $\frac{7}{15} = \frac{?}{45}$

22. $\frac{3}{22} = \frac{?}{44}$

23. $\frac{5}{16} = \frac{?}{32}$

24. $\frac{?}{19} = \frac{10}{38}$

Basic Computation Series 2000: Understanding Fractions
SECTION 1 Common Fractions, Equivalent Fractions, and Ratio and Proportion

Ratio and Proportion Word Problems

Solve each problem using a proportion.

1. A printing press can produce 20,000 newspapers in 5 hours. Working at the same rate, how many can be produced in 12 hours?

2. A boy 45 inches tall casts a shadow 90 inches long. At the same time, his father's shadow is 144 inches long. How tall is the boy's father?

3. If 17 pounds of candy costs $136, what would be the cost of 51 pounds of the same kind of candy?

4. The ratio of men to women in a meeting was $\frac{4}{5}$. How many men would be in a meeting where the ratio was the same and there were 20 women in the meeting?

Basic Computation Series 2000: Understanding Fractions
SECTION 1 Common Fractions, Equivalent Fractions, and Ratio and Proportion

39

Proportions

Use cross products to replace the ? with = or ≠ to make a true statement.

1. $\frac{4}{11}$? $\frac{12}{33}$

2. $\frac{8}{9}$? $\frac{56}{72}$

3. $\frac{3}{4}$? $\frac{81}{108}$

4. $\frac{5}{6}$? $\frac{32}{42}$

5. $\frac{2}{3}$? $\frac{14}{24}$

6. $\frac{4}{5}$? $\frac{16}{20}$

7. $\frac{9}{10}$? $\frac{18}{20}$

8. $\frac{1}{7}$? $\frac{5}{28}$

9. $\frac{7}{10}$? $\frac{5}{9}$

10. $\frac{3}{5}$? $\frac{9}{15}$

11. $\frac{12}{19}$? $\frac{24}{38}$

12. $\frac{24}{27}$? $\frac{9}{10}$

Complete each of the following by replacing the ? in each statement to make a proportion.

13. $\frac{?}{25} = \frac{2}{5}$

14. $\frac{?}{128} = \frac{11}{16}$

15. $\frac{?}{78} = \frac{9}{13}$

16. $\frac{?}{64} = \frac{6}{16}$

17. $\frac{35}{?} = \frac{7}{15}$

18. $\frac{27}{?} = \frac{9}{13}$

19. $\frac{?}{85} = \frac{9}{17}$

20. $\frac{24}{?} = \frac{8}{17}$

21. $\frac{26}{33} = \frac{?}{66}$

22. $\frac{5}{17} = \frac{?}{34}$

23. $\frac{7}{19} = \frac{21}{?}$

24. $\frac{4}{15} = \frac{?}{45}$

Ratio and Proportion Word Problems

Solve each problem using a proportion.

1. The ratio of males to females in a math class is $\frac{3}{4}$. If there are 12 males, how may females are there?

2. The price of bananas is 99 cents for four pounds. At the same price per pound, what is the cost of twelve pounds of bananas (in cents)?

3. A motorcycle driver travels 147 miles in 7 hours. Traveling at the same rate, how far would he travel in 10 hours?

4. The ratio of Patina's height to that of her mother is 3 to 5. If the mother is 65 inches tall, how tall is Patina?

Basic Computation Series 2000: Understanding Fractions
SECTION 1 Common Fractions, Equivalent Fractions, and Ratio and Proportion

41

Proportions

Use cross products to replace the ? with = or ≠ to make a true statement.

1. $\frac{3}{4}$? $\frac{27}{36}$

2. $\frac{2}{7}$? $\frac{24}{84}$

3. $\frac{5}{11}$? $\frac{25}{66}$

4. $\frac{3}{7}$? $\frac{30}{56}$

5. $\frac{4}{5}$? $\frac{32}{40}$

6. $\frac{3}{5}$? $\frac{27}{60}$

7. $\frac{7}{10}$? $\frac{42}{60}$

8. $\frac{5}{7}$? $\frac{35}{42}$

9. $\frac{22}{35}$? $\frac{14}{20}$

10. $\frac{16}{25}$? $\frac{80}{125}$

11. $\frac{7}{15}$? $\frac{10}{19}$

12. $\frac{4}{11}$? $\frac{16}{44}$

Complete each of the following by replacing the ? in each statement to make a proportion.

13. $\frac{80}{?} = \frac{10}{13}$

14. $\frac{?}{81} = \frac{26}{27}$

15. $\frac{77}{?} = \frac{11}{13}$

16. $\frac{63}{?} = \frac{7}{13}$

17. $\frac{?}{58} = \frac{12}{29}$

18. $\frac{39}{?} = \frac{3}{17}$

19. $\frac{27}{?} = \frac{9}{35}$

20. $\frac{32}{?} = \frac{16}{19}$

21. $\frac{17}{23} = \frac{51}{?}$

22. $\frac{16}{19} = \frac{?}{76}$

23. $\frac{?}{7} = \frac{20}{35}$

24. $\frac{?}{34} = \frac{8}{17}$

Basic Computation Series 2000: Understanding Fractions
SECTION 1 Common Fractions, Equivalent Fractions, and Ratio and Proportion

Ratio and Proportion Word Problems

Solve each problem using a proportion.

1. Steve traveled 13 miles on his bicycle in 2 hours. Riding at the same rate, how long would it take him to travel 39 miles?

2. The scale on a blueprint is 1 inch = 4 feet. If the shortest side of a house measures 13 inches on the blueprint, how long is this side of the actual house in feet?

3. Lamont High School is preparing for a picnic. They plan to have hamburgers and hot dogs in a ratio of 3 to 5. If they have 27 dozen hamburgers, how many hot dogs will they need?

4. A 28-inch snowfall that fell on the Loafman ranch had a moisture content of 2 inches. If at another time it snowed 56 inches with the same ratio of snow depth to moisture content, how many inches of moisture was there in the second snowfall?

Basic Computation Series 2000: Understanding Fractions
SECTION 1 Common Fractions, Equivalent Fractions, and Ratio and Proportion

43

Proportions

Use cross products to replace the ? with = or ≠ to make a true statement.

1. $\frac{2}{3}$? $\frac{24}{36}$

2. $\frac{7}{8}$? $\frac{49}{64}$

3. $\frac{5}{7}$? $\frac{30}{42}$

4. $\frac{4}{9}$? $\frac{16}{27}$

5. $\frac{3}{7}$? $\frac{42}{84}$

6. $\frac{3}{5}$? $\frac{15}{25}$

7. $\frac{3}{10}$? $\frac{9}{30}$

8. $\frac{5}{8}$? $\frac{25}{64}$

9. $\frac{2}{15}$? $\frac{3}{11}$

10. $\frac{17}{18}$? $\frac{34}{36}$

11. $\frac{2}{9}$? $\frac{3}{17}$

12. $\frac{7}{16}$? $\frac{21}{48}$

Complete each of the following by replacing the ? in each statement to make a proportion.

13. $\frac{?}{85} = \frac{4}{17}$

14. $\frac{16}{?} = \frac{4}{5}$

15. $\frac{15}{85} = \frac{?}{17}$

16. $\frac{4}{5} = \frac{12}{?}$

17. $\frac{27}{?} = \frac{9}{14}$

18. $\frac{?}{64} = \frac{2}{32}$

19. $\frac{12}{15} = \frac{?}{45}$

20. $\frac{28}{?} = \frac{7}{45}$

21. $\frac{?}{22} = \frac{12}{44}$

22. $\frac{?}{13} = \frac{42}{78}$

23. $\frac{15}{17} = \frac{?}{68}$

24. $\frac{35}{77} = \frac{?}{11}$

Basic Computation Series 2000: Understanding Fractions
SECTION 1 Common Fractions, Equivalent Fractions, and Ratio and Proportion

Ratio and Proportion Word Problems

Solve each problem using a proportion.

1. A stick 36 inches long casts a shadow 54 inches long at the same time a nearby pole casts a shadow 72 feet long. How tall is the pole?

2. The price of apples is three pounds for 87 cents. What is the cost of 12 pounds of apples?

3. The ratio of the time it takes a train to travel a certain distance to the time it takes a particular automobile to travel the same distance is 4 to 5. If the train travels 20 hours to reach St. Louis, how long would it take the automobile to reach the same destination over the same route?

4. The "Chili Egg Puff" recipe calls for Cheddar cheese and Monterey Jack cheese in a ratio of 3 to 4. If 9 cups of Cheddar cheese are used in a large version of the recipe, how many cups of Monterey Jack cheese would be used?

Basic Computation Series 2000: Understanding Fractions
SECTION 1 Common Fractions, Equivalent Fractions, and Ratio and Proportion

45

Least Common Denominator, Improper Fractions, and Mixed Numbers

In order to add or subtract fractions (skills which will be explored more thoroughly in Book 3, *Working with Fractions*), the fractions must have the same denominator. In problems of this sort, it may be necessary to determine fractions with the same denominator that are equivalent to the given fractions. The most efficient way to determine the denominator of the equivalent fractions is to find the *least common denominator* (LCD) of the two fractions. The LCD is the smallest number that is a multiple of each denominator.

To find the LCD of two or more fractions, first write each denominator in prime factored form. Then find the product of the prime factors of the denominators, with each factor written the maximum number of times it appears in *either* denominator.

Example 1: Find the LCD for each of the following pairs of fractions.

   a. $\frac{7}{15}$ and $\frac{3}{20}$

   b. $\frac{3}{25}$ and $\frac{7}{30}$

   c. $\frac{2}{3}$ and $\frac{3}{4}$

   d. $\frac{11}{16}$ and $\frac{7}{40}$

Solution: Write each denominator in prime factored form. Then "build" the LCD for each pair.

   a. $15 = 3 \times 5$; $20 = 2 \times 2 \times 5$. The LCD is $3 \times 5 \times 2^2$, which equals 60.

   b. $25 = 5 \times 5$; $30 = 2 \times 3 \times 5$. The LCD is $2 \times 3 \times 5^2$, which equals 150.

   c. 3 is a prime number; $4 = 2 \times 2$. The LCD is 3×2^2, which equals 12.

   d. $16 = 2 \times 2 \times 2 \times 2$; $40 = 2 \times 2 \times 2 \times 5$. The LCD is $2^4 \times 5$, which equals 80.

To compare or *order* two fractions, first find the LCD of the fractions. Then write fractions equivalent to the given fractions using the LCD as the denominators. Of the equivalent fractions, the one with lesser numerator is the lesser fraction.

Example 2: Circle the lesser fraction in each pair.

   a. $\frac{3}{4}$ and $\frac{5}{8}$

   b. $\frac{4}{7}$ and $\frac{5}{8}$

   c. $\frac{4}{15}$ and $\frac{7}{20}$

   d. $\frac{7}{10}$ and $\frac{8}{13}$

Solution:

   a. The LCD for $\frac{3}{4}$ and $\frac{5}{8}$ is 8. $\frac{3}{4} = \frac{6}{8}$ and $\frac{5}{8} = \frac{5}{8}$. Note that 5 is less than 6. Circle $\frac{5}{8}$.

   b. The LCD for $\frac{4}{7}$ and $\frac{5}{8}$ is 56. $\frac{4}{7} = \frac{32}{56}$ and $\frac{5}{8} = \frac{35}{56}$. Note that 32 is less than 35. Circle $\frac{4}{7}$.

   c. The LCD for $\frac{4}{15}$ and $\frac{7}{20}$ is 60. $\frac{4}{15} = \frac{16}{60}$ and $\frac{7}{20} = \frac{21}{60}$. Note that 16 is less than 21. Circle $\frac{4}{15}$.

   d. The LCD for $\frac{7}{10}$ and $\frac{8}{13}$ is 130. $\frac{7}{10} = \frac{91}{130}$ and $\frac{8}{13} = \frac{80}{130}$. Note that 80 is less than 91. Circle $\frac{8}{13}$.

An *improper* fraction is a fraction that represents a number that is greater than 1. The numerator of an improper fraction is larger than the denominator. For example, $\frac{7}{5}$ is an improper fraction.

An improper fraction can be written as a *mixed number*. A mixed number has two parts, a whole number part and a fractional part, with an implied addition sign between them. For example, $\frac{7}{5} = 1\frac{2}{5}$, which means $\frac{7}{5} = 1 + \frac{2}{5}$. When reading a mixed number, the implied addition sign is read as "and." The mixed number $1\frac{2}{5}$ is read as "one and $\frac{2}{5}$".

To write an improper fraction as a mixed number, divide the denominator into the numerator to find the whole number part of the mixed number. Write the remainder over the denominator to find the fractional part of the mixed number. For example, to write $\frac{7}{5}$ as a mixed number, divide 7 by 5. $7 \div 5 = 1$ remainder 2. Therefore, $\frac{7}{5} = 1\frac{2}{5}$.

As was true for common fractions, an improper fraction is reduced to *lowest terms* when the GCF of the numerator and denominator is 1. A mixed number is in *simplest form* if the fractional part is a common fraction reduced to lowest terms.

Example 3: Write each of the following as a mixed number in simplest form.

   a. $\frac{10}{7}$ **c.** $\frac{30}{17}$

   b. $\frac{54}{15}$ **d.** $\frac{21}{6}$

Solution:

   a. $10 \div 7 = 1$ remainder 3. $\frac{10}{7} = 1\frac{3}{7}$. The GCF of 3 and 7 is 1; therefore, $1\frac{3}{7}$ is in simplest form.

Basic Computation Series 2000: Understanding Fractions
SECTION 2 Least Common Denominator, Improper Fractions, and Mixed Numbers

47

b. $54 \div 15 = 3$ remainder 9. $\frac{54}{15} = 3\frac{9}{15}$. The GCF of 9 and 15 is 3; therefore, the fractional part of the answer will need to be reduced by dividing the numerator and denominator by 3. In simplest form, $\frac{54}{15} = 3\frac{3}{5}$.

c. $30 \div 17 = 1$ remainder 13. $\frac{30}{17} = 1\frac{13}{17}$. The GCF of 13 and 17 is 1; therefore, $1\frac{13}{17}$ is in simplest form.

d. $21 \div 6 = 3$ remainder 3. $\frac{21}{6} = 3\frac{3}{6}$. The GCF of 3 and 6 is 3; therefore, the fractional part of the answer will need to be reduced by dividing the numerator and denominator by 3. In simplest form, $\frac{21}{6} = 3\frac{1}{2}$.

To write a mixed number as an improper fraction, follow these steps:

   i. Multiply the denominator of the fractional part by the whole number part of the mixed number.

   ii. Add the numerator of the fractional part of the mixed number to your product.

   iii. Write a fraction using your result as the numerator, and the denominator of the fractional part of the original mixed number as the denominator.

Example 4: Rewrite the following mixed numbers as improper fractions.

   a. $2\frac{4}{15}$ **c.** $5\frac{3}{8}$

   b. $7\frac{2}{3}$ **d.** $10\frac{2}{3}$

Solution: **a.** To get the numerator of the desired improper fraction, multiply 15 by 2 and add 4 to the result. Use the original denominator, 15, for the denominator. $2\frac{4}{15} = \frac{34}{15}$

            b. To get the numerator of the desired improper fraction, multiply 3 by 7 and add 2 to the result. Use the original denominator, 3, for the denominator. $7\frac{2}{3} = \frac{23}{3}$

            c. To get the numerator of the desired improper fraction, multiply 8 by 5 and add 3 to the result. Use the original denominator, 8, for the denominator. $5\frac{3}{8} = \frac{43}{8}$

            d. To get the numerator of the desired improper fraction, multiply 3 by 10 and add 2 to the result. Use the original denominator, 3, for the denominator. $10\frac{2}{3} = \frac{32}{3}$

Example 5: Write $4\frac{15}{10}$ as a mixed number in simplest form.

Solution: In simplest form, the fractional part of a mixed number must be a common fraction reduced to lowest terms. $\frac{15}{10} = 1\frac{5}{10} = 1\frac{1}{2}$. Therefore, the original mixed number is $4 + 1 + \frac{1}{2}$, which is $5\frac{1}{2}$.

Basic Computation Series 2000: Understanding Fractions
SECTION 2 Least Common Denominator, Improper Fractions, and Mixed Numbers

Least Common Denominator

Find the least common denominator for each pair of fractions.

1. $\frac{1}{4}$, $\frac{1}{5}$ ___20___	**9.** $\frac{5}{16}$, $\frac{7}{12}$ _____	**17.** $\frac{4}{15}$, $\frac{7}{40}$ _____
2. $\frac{5}{12}$, $\frac{7}{18}$ _____	**10.** $\frac{1}{14}$, $\frac{7}{20}$ _____	**18.** $\frac{13}{28}$, $\frac{17}{35}$ _____
3. $\frac{2}{5}$, $\frac{5}{7}$ _____	**11.** $\frac{13}{16}$, $\frac{9}{44}$ _____	**19.** $\frac{3}{10}$, $\frac{7}{15}$ _____
4. $\frac{5}{6}$, $\frac{6}{7}$ _____	**12.** $\frac{5}{18}$, $\frac{13}{27}$ _____	**20.** $\frac{7}{36}$, $\frac{11}{27}$ _____
5. $\frac{7}{10}$, $\frac{11}{12}$ _____	**13.** $\frac{3}{14}$, $\frac{5}{21}$ _____	**21.** $\frac{19}{42}$, $\frac{6}{35}$ _____
6. $\frac{1}{4}$, $\frac{7}{20}$ _____	**14.** $\frac{11}{16}$, $\frac{9}{20}$ _____	**22.** $\frac{7}{22}$, $\frac{13}{55}$ _____
7. $\frac{2}{3}$, $\frac{1}{2}$ _____	**15.** $\frac{6}{25}$, $\frac{7}{30}$ _____	**23.** $\frac{5}{32}$, $\frac{11}{40}$ _____
8. $\frac{4}{9}$, $\frac{7}{18}$ _____	**16.** $\frac{7}{24}$, $\frac{9}{40}$ _____	**24.** $\frac{7}{36}$, $\frac{13}{48}$ _____

Ordering Fractions

Circle the lesser fraction in each pair.

1. ⓵⁄₃ , $\frac{3}{8}$	11. $\frac{5}{7}$, $\frac{9}{14}$	21. $\frac{5}{8}$, $\frac{7}{9}$
2. $\frac{1}{4}$, $\frac{5}{16}$	12. $\frac{3}{5}$, $\frac{5}{10}$	22. $\frac{4}{7}$, $\frac{9}{14}$
3. $\frac{1}{2}$, $\frac{2}{8}$	13. $\frac{5}{9}$, $\frac{13}{18}$	23. $\frac{3}{8}$, $\frac{5}{16}$
4. $\frac{9}{16}$, $\frac{5}{8}$	14. $\frac{8}{10}$, $\frac{15}{20}$	24. $\frac{2}{5}$, $\frac{3}{7}$
5. $\frac{4}{5}$, $\frac{13}{15}$	15. $\frac{2}{3}$, $\frac{3}{4}$	25. $\frac{7}{8}$, $\frac{11}{12}$
6. $\frac{1}{2}$, $\frac{1}{3}$	16. $\frac{3}{4}$, $\frac{7}{8}$	26. $\frac{1}{6}$, $\frac{1}{9}$
7. $\frac{3}{10}$, $\frac{1}{5}$	17. $\frac{1}{2}$, $\frac{3}{8}$	27. $\frac{5}{9}$, $\frac{5}{12}$
8. $\frac{2}{16}$, $\frac{1}{7}$	18. $\frac{3}{8}$, $\frac{1}{4}$	28. $\frac{3}{5}$, $\frac{7}{15}$
9. $\frac{5}{12}$, $\frac{2}{7}$	19. $\frac{3}{11}$, $\frac{2}{9}$	29. $\frac{3}{16}$, $\frac{5}{9}$
10. $\frac{9}{13}$, $\frac{3}{7}$	20. $\frac{4}{9}$, $\frac{3}{5}$	30. $\frac{7}{13}$, $\frac{5}{8}$

Basic Computation Series 2000: Understanding Fractions
SECTION 2 Least Common Denominator, Improper Fractions, and Mixed Numbers

Least Common Denominator

Find the least common denominator for each pair of fractions.

1. $\frac{1}{2}$, $\frac{1}{3}$ ____6____

2. $\frac{2}{3}$, $\frac{3}{5}$ _____

3. $\frac{3}{8}$, $\frac{7}{12}$ _____

4. $\frac{1}{4}$, $\frac{5}{6}$ _____

5. $\frac{3}{10}$, $\frac{7}{15}$ _____

6. $\frac{3}{10}$, $\frac{5}{16}$ _____

7. $\frac{1}{2}$, $\frac{1}{4}$ _____

8. $\frac{3}{4}$, $\frac{5}{12}$ _____

9. $\frac{7}{16}$, $\frac{9}{20}$ _____

10. $\frac{11}{12}$, $\frac{11}{20}$ _____

11. $\frac{3}{10}$, $\frac{7}{18}$ _____

12. $\frac{3}{9}$, $\frac{7}{15}$ _____

13. $\frac{1}{6}$, $\frac{1}{3}$ _____

14. $\frac{1}{2}$, $\frac{3}{8}$ _____

15. $\frac{7}{15}$, $\frac{7}{18}$ _____

16. $\frac{1}{4}$, $\frac{3}{14}$ _____

17. $\frac{5}{8}$, $\frac{9}{20}$ _____

18. $\frac{5}{12}$, $\frac{13}{18}$ _____

19. $\frac{1}{6}$, $\frac{1}{8}$ _____

20. $\frac{5}{9}$, $\frac{7}{12}$ _____

21. $\frac{9}{20}$, $\frac{13}{30}$ _____

22. $\frac{7}{15}$, $\frac{11}{25}$ _____

23. $\frac{7}{18}$, $\frac{11}{24}$ _____

24. $\frac{4}{25}$, $\frac{9}{35}$ _____

Basic Computation Series 2000: Understanding Fractions
SECTION 2 Least Common Denominator, Improper Fractions, and Mixed Numbers

51

Ordering Fractions

Circle the lesser fraction in each pair.

1. $\frac{7}{11}$, $\boxed{\frac{13}{22}}$	**11.** $\frac{5}{16}$, $\frac{17}{24}$	**21.** $\frac{16}{27}$, $\frac{17}{36}$
2. $\frac{3}{4}$, $\frac{2}{3}$	**12.** $\frac{7}{15}$, $\frac{3}{5}$	**22.** $\frac{3}{25}$, $\frac{11}{100}$
3. $\frac{1}{3}$, $\frac{9}{25}$	**13.** $\frac{1}{10}$, $\frac{3}{8}$	**23.** $\frac{1}{2}$, $\frac{5}{8}$
4. $\frac{4}{9}$, $\frac{1}{2}$	**14.** $\frac{1}{2}$, $\frac{31}{64}$	**24.** $\frac{3}{50}$, $\frac{3}{25}$
5. $\frac{5}{7}$, $\frac{7}{12}$	**15.** $\frac{5}{6}$, $\frac{7}{8}$	**25.** $\frac{11}{13}$, $\frac{10}{11}$
6. $\frac{1}{7}$, $\frac{1}{8}$	**16.** $\frac{6}{7}$, $\frac{3}{11}$	**26.** $\frac{1}{3}$, $\frac{3}{8}$
7. $\frac{1}{3}$, $\frac{3}{4}$	**17.** $\frac{1}{5}$, $\frac{1}{7}$	**27.** $\frac{5}{6}$, $\frac{7}{18}$
8. $\frac{7}{10}$, $\frac{3}{7}$	**18.** $\frac{5}{13}$, $\frac{4}{5}$	**28.** $\frac{3}{4}$, $\frac{7}{12}$
9. $\frac{7}{20}$, $\frac{3}{5}$	**19.** $\frac{3}{11}$, $\frac{1}{4}$	**29.** $\frac{2}{3}$, $\frac{4}{15}$
10. $\frac{7}{12}$, $\frac{1}{2}$	**20.** $\frac{5}{7}$, $\frac{4}{9}$	**30.** $\frac{7}{16}$, $\frac{5}{12}$

Basic Computation Series 2000: Understanding Fractions
SECTION 2 Least Common Denominator, Improper Fractions, and Mixed Numbers

Least Common Denominator

Find the least common denominator for each pair of fractions.

1. $\frac{3}{4}$, $\frac{5}{6}$ _____12_____

2. $\frac{6}{13}$, $\frac{7}{39}$ _____

3. $\frac{11}{16}$, $\frac{25}{64}$ _____

4. $\frac{1}{2}$, $\frac{7}{20}$ _____

5. $\frac{7}{10}$, $\frac{4}{15}$ _____

6. $\frac{5}{6}$, $\frac{9}{25}$ _____

7. $\frac{2}{5}$, $\frac{5}{7}$ _____

8. $\frac{16}{34}$, $\frac{19}{51}$ _____

9. $\frac{7}{9}$, $\frac{2}{3}$ _____

10. $\frac{3}{5}$, $\frac{7}{9}$ _____

11. $\frac{1}{4}$, $\frac{3}{11}$ _____

12. $\frac{7}{16}$, $\frac{13}{24}$ _____

13. $\frac{7}{12}$, $\frac{8}{15}$ _____

14. $\frac{15}{22}$, $\frac{17}{33}$ _____

15. $\frac{3}{17}$, $\frac{14}{85}$ _____

16. $\frac{7}{10}$, $\frac{5}{12}$ _____

17. $\frac{5}{8}$, $\frac{9}{32}$ _____

18. $\frac{4}{5}$, $\frac{7}{15}$ _____

19. $\frac{7}{10}$, $\frac{11}{16}$ _____

20. $\frac{5}{7}$, $\frac{2}{3}$ _____

21. $\frac{5}{13}$, $\frac{9}{91}$ _____

22. $\frac{3}{4}$, $\frac{9}{16}$ _____

23. $\frac{11}{12}$, $\frac{7}{20}$ _____

24. $\frac{3}{8}$, $\frac{5}{13}$ _____

Basic Computation Series 2000: Understanding Fractions
SECTION 2 Least Common Denominator, Improper Fractions, and Mixed Numbers

53

Ordering Fractions

Circle the lesser fraction in each pair.

1. $\frac{7}{19}$, $\left(\frac{20}{57}\right)$	**11.** $\frac{3}{12}$, $\frac{17}{30}$	**21.** $\frac{4}{9}$, $\frac{27}{45}$
2. $\frac{9}{12}$, $\frac{15}{24}$	**12.** $\frac{2}{3}$, $\frac{7}{15}$	**22.** $\frac{7}{9}$, $\frac{15}{18}$
3. $\frac{9}{12}$, $\frac{7}{8}$	**13.** $\frac{2}{6}$, $\frac{2}{12}$	**23.** $\frac{3}{7}$, $\frac{8}{21}$
4. $\frac{7}{13}$, $\frac{15}{23}$	**14.** $\frac{3}{8}$, $\frac{8}{24}$	**24.** $\frac{5}{6}$, $\frac{13}{18}$
5. $\frac{4}{5}$, $\frac{15}{20}$	**15.** $\frac{5}{7}$, $\frac{21}{28}$	**25.** $\frac{4}{6}$, $\frac{15}{24}$
6. $\frac{9}{10}$, $\frac{2}{3}$	**16.** $\frac{2}{5}$, $\frac{3}{8}$	**26.** $\frac{3}{4}$, $\frac{7}{16}$
7. $\frac{1}{8}$, $\frac{1}{10}$	**17.** $\frac{7}{16}$, $\frac{3}{8}$	**27.** $\frac{5}{6}$, $\frac{7}{9}$
8. $\frac{11}{12}$, $\frac{3}{4}$	**18.** $\frac{7}{13}$, $\frac{3}{10}$	**28.** $\frac{7}{8}$, $\frac{11}{16}$
9. $\frac{2}{9}$, $\frac{3}{8}$	**19.** $\frac{11}{12}$, $\frac{5}{6}$	**29.** $\frac{4}{5}$, $\frac{7}{15}$
10. $\frac{3}{20}$, $\frac{2}{9}$	**20.** $\frac{4}{15}$, $\frac{7}{20}$	**30.** $\frac{16}{17}$, $\frac{4}{5}$

54

Basic Computation Series 2000: Understanding Fractions
SECTION 2 Least Common Denominator, Improper Fractions, and Mixed Numbers

Least Common Denominator

Find the least common denominator for each pair of fractions.

1. $\frac{3}{7}$, $\frac{5}{14}$ ____14____

2. $\frac{17}{32}$, $\frac{9}{40}$ _____

3. $\frac{5}{36}$, $\frac{7}{45}$ _____

4. $\frac{7}{8}$, $\frac{3}{14}$ _____

5. $\frac{3}{8}$, $\frac{5}{12}$ _____

6. $\frac{9}{10}$, $\frac{4}{15}$ _____

7. $\frac{7}{8}$, $\frac{9}{14}$ _____

8. $\frac{12}{25}$, $\frac{7}{20}$ _____

9. $\frac{13}{21}$, $\frac{7}{33}$ _____

10. $\frac{9}{10}$, $\frac{5}{12}$ _____

11. $\frac{7}{12}$, $\frac{13}{15}$ _____

12. $\frac{3}{4}$, $\frac{7}{30}$ _____

13. $\frac{20}{21}$, $\frac{8}{27}$ _____

14. $\frac{8}{25}$, $\frac{7}{10}$ _____

15. $\frac{7}{13}$, $\frac{5}{39}$ _____

16. $\frac{5}{14}$, $\frac{13}{21}$ _____

17. $\frac{1}{6}$, $\frac{7}{16}$ _____

18. $\frac{3}{8}$, $\frac{9}{16}$ _____

19. $\frac{5}{36}$, $\frac{11}{40}$ _____

20. $\frac{23}{24}$, $\frac{9}{16}$ _____

21. $\frac{11}{17}$, $\frac{6}{51}$ _____

22. $\frac{4}{9}$, $\frac{7}{12}$ _____

23. $\frac{4}{9}$, $\frac{7}{15}$ _____

24. $\frac{1}{4}$, $\frac{5}{12}$ _____

Ordering Fractions

Circle the lesser fraction in each pair.

1. $\frac{7}{13}$, $\boxed{\frac{9}{26}}$	**11.** $\frac{8}{15}$, $\frac{7}{25}$	**21.** $\frac{16}{27}$, $\frac{17}{36}$
2. $\frac{1}{2}$, $\frac{1}{5}$	**12.** $\frac{1}{5}$, $\frac{1}{3}$	**22.** $\frac{5}{8}$, $\frac{2}{3}$
3. $\frac{2}{3}$, $\frac{3}{5}$	**13.** $\frac{1}{4}$, $\frac{5}{16}$	**23.** $\frac{5}{16}$, $\frac{3}{8}$
4. $\frac{2}{3}$, $\frac{11}{16}$	**14.** $\frac{11}{16}$, $\frac{17}{20}$	**24.** $\frac{1}{2}$, $\frac{3}{7}$
5. $\frac{3}{8}$, $\frac{4}{9}$	**15.** $\frac{7}{16}$, $\frac{5}{12}$	**25.** $\frac{8}{11}$, $\frac{9}{13}$
6. $\frac{1}{11}$, $\frac{1}{14}$	**16.** $\frac{4}{7}$, $\frac{3}{5}$	**26.** $\frac{21}{25}$, $\frac{7}{10}$
7. $\frac{5}{16}$, $\frac{2}{5}$	**17.** $\frac{11}{10}$, $\frac{3}{5}$	**27.** $\frac{3}{5}$, $\frac{5}{6}$
8. $\frac{2}{3}$, $\frac{4}{7}$	**18.** $\frac{3}{5}$, $\frac{5}{7}$	**28.** $\frac{7}{13}$, $\frac{11}{26}$
9. $\frac{3}{7}$, $\frac{5}{8}$	**19.** $\frac{7}{9}$, $\frac{6}{7}$	**29.** $\frac{11}{12}$, $\frac{8}{9}$
10. $\frac{11}{20}$, $\frac{5}{6}$	**20.** $\frac{5}{13}$, $\frac{11}{15}$	**30.** $\frac{13}{20}$, $\frac{7}{12}$

Basic Computation Series 2000: Understanding Fractions
SECTION 2 Least Common Denominator, Improper Fractions, and Mixed Numbers

Least Common Denominator

Find the least common denominator for each pair of fractions.

1. $\frac{1}{2}$, $\frac{1}{3}$ ___6___

2. $\frac{4}{9}$, $\frac{7}{18}$ _____

3. $\frac{3}{8}$, $\frac{5}{12}$ _____

4. $\frac{5}{8}$, $\frac{7}{13}$ _____

5. $\frac{3}{4}$, $\frac{13}{20}$ _____

6. $\frac{5}{6}$, $\frac{13}{15}$ _____

7. $\frac{1}{3}$, $\frac{1}{6}$ _____

8. $\frac{3}{4}$, $\frac{7}{16}$ _____

9. $\frac{5}{8}$, $\frac{1}{6}$ _____

10. $\frac{3}{4}$, $\frac{8}{11}$ _____

11. $\frac{1}{6}$, $\frac{5}{16}$ _____

12. $\frac{1}{4}$, $\frac{7}{13}$ _____

13. $\frac{2}{3}$, $\frac{4}{5}$ _____

14. $\frac{7}{12}$, $\frac{2}{3}$ _____

15. $\frac{5}{7}$, $\frac{3}{5}$ _____

16. $\frac{3}{10}$, $\frac{11}{25}$ _____

17. $\frac{3}{5}$, $\frac{9}{25}$ _____

18. $\frac{11}{12}$, $\frac{5}{36}$ _____

19. $\frac{3}{16}$, $\frac{1}{12}$ _____

20. $\frac{2}{3}$, $\frac{11}{15}$ _____

21. $\frac{7}{10}$, $\frac{2}{3}$ _____

22. $\frac{7}{16}$, $\frac{29}{32}$ _____

23. $\frac{1}{3}$, $\frac{10}{11}$ _____

24. $\frac{7}{9}$, $\frac{13}{27}$ _____

Basic Computation Series 2000: Understanding Fractions
SECTION 2 Least Common Denominator, Improper Fractions, and Mixed Numbers

57

Ordering Fractions

Circle the lesser fraction in each pair.

1. $\boxed{\frac{9}{16}}$, $\frac{5}{8}$	11. $\frac{5}{7}$, $\frac{9}{14}$	21. $\frac{8}{10}$, $\frac{15}{20}$
2. $\frac{7}{15}$, $\frac{3}{5}$	12. $\frac{1}{2}$, $\frac{5}{8}$	22. $\frac{33}{64}$, $\frac{1}{2}$
3. $\frac{1}{4}$, $\frac{1}{2}$	13. $\frac{1}{2}$, $\frac{1}{5}$	23. $\frac{7}{8}$, $\frac{8}{9}$
4. $\frac{9}{10}$, $\frac{4}{5}$	14. $\frac{5}{7}$, $\frac{3}{5}$	24. $\frac{2}{3}$, $\frac{5}{8}$
5. $\frac{4}{7}$, $\frac{3}{8}$	15. $\frac{2}{5}$, $\frac{5}{16}$	25. $\frac{7}{9}$, $\frac{13}{18}$
6. $\frac{1}{4}$, $\frac{3}{9}$	16. $\frac{11}{20}$, $\frac{7}{15}$	26. $\frac{6}{11}$, $\frac{7}{10}$
7. $\frac{1}{9}$, $\frac{1}{10}$	17. $\frac{3}{16}$, $\frac{5}{11}$	27. $\frac{14}{15}$, $\frac{5}{12}$
8. $\frac{2}{3}$, $\frac{6}{7}$	18. $\frac{3}{8}$, $\frac{5}{12}$	28. $\frac{3}{4}$, $\frac{5}{8}$
9. $\frac{2}{11}$, $\frac{5}{13}$	19. $\frac{4}{5}$, $\frac{7}{10}$	29. $\frac{6}{7}$, $\frac{11}{21}$
10. $\frac{7}{11}$, $\frac{5}{9}$	20. $\frac{5}{8}$, $\frac{6}{7}$	30. $\frac{11}{13}$, $\frac{6}{7}$

58

Basic Computation Series 2000: Understanding Fractions
SECTION 2 Least Common Denominator, Improper Fractions, and Mixed Numbers

Mixed Numbers and Improper Fractions

Rewrite each improper fraction as a mixed number in lowest terms.

1. $\frac{19}{16} = 1\frac{3}{16}$

2. $\frac{23}{17} = $ _____

3. $\frac{28}{15} = $ _____

4. $\frac{38}{17} = $ _____

5. $\frac{35}{18} = $ _____

6. $\frac{40}{19} = $ _____

7. $\frac{36}{29} = $ _____

8. $\frac{50}{31} = $ _____

9. $\frac{43}{17} = $ _____

10. $\frac{72}{35} = $ _____

11. $\frac{15}{8} = $ _____

12. $\frac{16}{9} = $ _____

Rewrite each mixed number as an improper fraction.

13. $1\frac{3}{4} = \frac{7}{4}$

14. $10\frac{5}{8} = $ _____

15. $6\frac{1}{2} = $ _____

16. $8\frac{2}{3} = $ _____

17. $9\frac{1}{5} = $ _____

18. $5\frac{3}{5} = $ _____

19. $6\frac{2}{3} = $ _____

20. $8\frac{3}{5} = $ _____

21. $6\frac{1}{3} = $ _____

22. $5\frac{3}{4} = $ _____

23. $2\frac{1}{2} = $ _____

24. $9\frac{1}{8} = $ _____

Basic Computation Series 2000: Understanding Fractions
SECTION 2 Least Common Denominator, Improper Fractions, and Mixed Numbers

59

Simplifying Mixed Numbers

Rewrite each of the following as a mixed number in simplest form or as a whole number.

1. $3\frac{40}{9} =$ ___ $7\frac{4}{9}$ ___

2. $12\frac{25}{10} =$ _____

3. $7\frac{18}{15} =$ _____

4. $5\frac{13}{2} =$ _____

5. $7\frac{12}{9} =$ _____

6. $18\frac{28}{14} =$ _____

7. $10\frac{27}{6} =$ _____

8. $8\frac{11}{3} =$ _____

9. $5\frac{9}{2} =$ _____

10. $6\frac{12}{8} =$ _____

11. $13\frac{5}{4} =$ _____

12. $6\frac{23}{7} =$ _____

13. $8\frac{10}{4} =$ _____

14. $7\frac{10}{8} =$ _____

15. $9\frac{50}{10} =$ _____

16. $1\frac{33}{8} =$ _____

Basic Computation Series 2000: Understanding Fractions
SECTION 2 Least Common Denominator, Improper Fractions, and Mixed Numbers

Mixed Numbers and Improper Fractions

Rewrite each improper fraction as a mixed number in lowest terms.

1. $\frac{24}{16} = \underline{1\frac{1}{2}}$

7. $\frac{55}{32} = \underline{\hphantom{xxxx}}$

2. $\frac{74}{20} = \underline{\hphantom{xxxx}}$

8. $\frac{35}{4} = \underline{\hphantom{xxxx}}$

3. $\frac{98}{47} = \underline{\hphantom{xxxx}}$

9. $\frac{29}{8} = \underline{\hphantom{xxxx}}$

4. $\frac{74}{33} = \underline{\hphantom{xxxx}}$

10. $\frac{54}{13} = \underline{\hphantom{xxxx}}$

5. $\frac{47}{20} = \underline{\hphantom{xxxx}}$

11. $\frac{18}{7} = \underline{\hphantom{xxxx}}$

6. $\frac{39}{19} = \underline{\hphantom{xxxx}}$

12. $\frac{29}{11} = \underline{\hphantom{xxxx}}$

Rewrite each mixed number as an improper fraction.

13. $5\frac{5}{6} = \underline{\frac{35}{6}}$

19. $7\frac{4}{5} = \underline{\hphantom{xxxx}}$

14. $7\frac{4}{9} = \underline{\hphantom{xxxx}}$

20. $3\frac{3}{8} = \underline{\hphantom{xxxx}}$

15. $12\frac{3}{7} = \underline{\hphantom{xxxx}}$

21. $2\frac{3}{4} = \underline{\hphantom{xxxx}}$

16. $6\frac{5}{8} = \underline{\hphantom{xxxx}}$

22. $4\frac{2}{3} = \underline{\hphantom{xxxx}}$

17. $4\frac{7}{9} = \underline{\hphantom{xxxx}}$

23. $16\frac{3}{5} = \underline{\hphantom{xxxx}}$

18. $15\frac{1}{2} = \underline{\hphantom{xxxx}}$

24. $4\frac{5}{6} = \underline{\hphantom{xxxx}}$

Basic Computation Series 2000: Understanding Fractions
SECTION 2 Least Common Denominator, Improper Fractions, and Mixed Numbers

61

Simplifying Mixed Numbers

Rewrite each of the following as a mixed number in simplest form or as a whole number.

1. $7\frac{21}{18}$ = _____ $8\frac{1}{6}$ _____

2. $15\frac{20}{6}$ = _____

3. $3\frac{14}{6}$ = _____

4. $11\frac{19}{3}$ = _____

5. $5\frac{11}{4}$ = _____

6. $48\frac{48}{15}$ = _____

7. $14\frac{28}{7}$ = _____

8. $2\frac{29}{4}$ = _____

9. $14\frac{39}{6}$ = _____

10. $17\frac{28}{20}$ = _____

11. $4\frac{12}{5}$ = _____

12. $5\frac{11}{2}$ = _____

13. $25\frac{29}{5}$ = _____

14. $15\frac{21}{14}$ = _____

15. $13\frac{21}{9}$ = _____

16. $15\frac{15}{11}$ = _____

Basic Computation Series 2000: Understanding Fractions
SECTION 2 Least Common Denominator, Improper Fractions, and Mixed Numbers

Mixed Numbers and Improper Fractions

Rewrite each improper fraction as a mixed number in lowest terms.

1. $\frac{201}{25} = 8\frac{1}{25}$

2. $\frac{158}{9} = $ _____

3. $\frac{132}{65} = $ _____

4. $\frac{170}{51} = $ _____

5. $\frac{39}{16} = $ _____

6. $\frac{115}{11} = $ _____

7. $\frac{98}{15} = $ _____

8. $\frac{47}{14} = $ _____

9. $\frac{82}{5} = $ _____

10. $\frac{119}{4} = $ _____

11. $\frac{67}{3} = $ _____

12. $\frac{481}{3} = $ _____

Rewrite each mixed number as an improper fraction.

13. $7\frac{4}{5} = \frac{39}{5}$

14. $4\frac{7}{8} = $ _____

15. $7\frac{1}{5} = $ _____

16. $9\frac{3}{8} = $ _____

17. $4\frac{7}{9} = $ _____

18. $15\frac{1}{2} = $ _____

19. $4\frac{3}{5} = $ _____

20. $6\frac{5}{8} = $ _____

21. $2\frac{9}{11} = $ _____

22. $7\frac{5}{8} = $ _____

23. $12\frac{3}{4} = $ _____

24. $3\frac{1}{2} = $ _____

Basic Computation Series 2000: Understanding Fractions
SECTION 2 Least Common Denominator, Improper Fractions, and Mixed Numbers

63

NAME

DATE

Simplifying Mixed Numbers

Rewrite each of the following as a mixed number in simplest form or as a whole number.

1. $50\frac{9}{2}$ = _____ $54\frac{1}{2}$ _____

2. $3\frac{9}{5}$ = _____

3. $7\frac{31}{3}$ = _____

4. $23\frac{17}{4}$ = _____

5. $12\frac{15}{6}$ = _____

6. $5\frac{26}{6}$ = _____

7. $12\frac{28}{10}$ = _____

8. $16\frac{14}{8}$ = _____

9. $24\frac{39}{14}$ = _____

10. $25\frac{38}{12}$ = _____

11. $9\frac{37}{6}$ = _____

12. $11\frac{16}{7}$ = _____

13. $6\frac{15}{3}$ = _____

14. $16\frac{93}{4}$ = _____

15. $6\frac{34}{5}$ = _____

16. $8\frac{19}{2}$ = _____

Basic Computation Series 2000: Understanding Fractions
SECTION 2 Least Common Denominator, Improper Fractions, and Mixed Numbers

Mixed Numbers and Improper Fractions

Rewrite each improper fraction as a mixed number in lowest terms.

1. $\frac{172}{5} = \underline{34\frac{2}{5}}$

7. $\frac{59}{14} = $ _____

2. $\frac{283}{6} = $ _____

8. $\frac{390}{23} = $ _____

3. $\frac{531}{25} = $ _____

9. $\frac{583}{15} = $ _____

4. $\frac{362}{5} = $ _____

10. $\frac{731}{12} = $ _____

5. $\frac{361}{8} = $ _____

11. $\frac{146}{5} = $ _____

6. $\frac{273}{10} = $ _____

12. $\frac{231}{8} = $ _____

Rewrite each mixed number as an improper fraction.

13. $7\frac{1}{9} = \underline{\frac{64}{9}}$

19. $5\frac{3}{4} = $ _____

14. $6\frac{4}{5} = $ _____

20. $6\frac{7}{9} = $ _____

15. $9\frac{2}{3} = $ _____

21. $13\frac{1}{2} = $ _____

16. $6\frac{3}{8} = $ _____

22. $23\frac{2}{3} = $ _____

17. $2\frac{2}{5} = $ _____

23. $8\frac{3}{16} = $ _____

18. $11\frac{1}{5} = $ _____

24. $4\frac{7}{12} = $ _____

Basic Computation Series 2000: Understanding Fractions
SECTION 2 Least Common Denominator, Improper Fractions, and Mixed Numbers

65

Simplifying Mixed Numbers

Rewrite each of the following as a mixed number in simplest form or as a whole number.

1. $7\frac{9}{4} =$ _____ $9\frac{1}{4}$ _____	**9.** $15\frac{16}{3} =$ _____
2. $21\frac{13}{7} =$ _____	**10.** $4\frac{9}{6} =$ _____
3. $10\frac{37}{7} =$ _____	**11.** $4\frac{47}{4} =$ _____
4. $1\frac{42}{5} =$ _____	**12.** $37\frac{18}{8} =$ _____
5. $5\frac{20}{4} =$ _____	**13.** $3\frac{50}{4} =$ _____
6. $3\frac{29}{18} =$ _____	**14.** $5\frac{12}{4} =$ _____
7. $2\frac{10}{2} =$ _____	**15.** $50\frac{12}{6} =$ _____
8. $32\frac{31}{9} =$ _____	**16.** $16\frac{10}{3} =$ _____

Basic Computation Series 2000: Understanding Fractions
SECTION 2 Least Common Denominator, Improper Fractions, and Mixed Numbers

Mixed Numbers and Improper Fractions

Rewrite each improper fraction as a mixed number in lowest terms.

1. $\frac{129}{5} = \underline{25\frac{4}{5}}$

2. $\frac{138}{6} = $ _____

3. $\frac{152}{7} = $ _____

4. $\frac{293}{8} = $ _____

5. $\frac{273}{5} = $ _____

6. $\frac{151}{30} = $ _____

7. $\frac{362}{25} = $ _____

8. $\frac{532}{12} = $ _____

9. $\frac{281}{13} = $ _____

10. $\frac{392}{15} = $ _____

11. $\frac{142}{13} = $ _____

12. $\frac{233}{11} = $ _____

Rewrite each mixed number as an improper fraction.

13. $6\frac{3}{5} = \underline{\frac{33}{5}}$

14. $2\frac{5}{9} = $ _____

15. $6\frac{5}{6} = $ _____

16. $3\frac{2}{3} = $ _____

17. $8\frac{1}{5} = $ _____

18. $10\frac{3}{4} = $ _____

19. $6\frac{1}{2} = $ _____

20. $3\frac{3}{7} = $ _____

21. $6\frac{1}{3} = $ _____

22. $12\frac{5}{9} = $ _____

23. $7\frac{5}{9} = $ _____

24. $12\frac{3}{4} = $ _____

Basic Computation Series 2000: Understanding Fractions
SECTION 2 Least Common Denominator, Improper Fractions, and Mixed Numbers

67

Simplifying Mixed Numbers

Rewrite each of the following as a mixed number in simplest form or as a whole number.

1. $5\frac{12}{5} = $ _____$7\frac{2}{5}$_____	**9.** $2\frac{12}{8} = $ _____
2. $3\frac{9}{6} = $ _____	**10.** $3\frac{28}{12} = $ _____
3. $12\frac{25}{10} = $ _____	**11.** $9\frac{35}{6} = $ _____
4. $11\frac{17}{4} = $ _____	**12.** $16\frac{10}{3} = $ _____
5. $4\frac{48}{10} = $ _____	**13.** $9\frac{27}{6} = $ _____
6. $10\frac{12}{7} = $ _____	**14.** $2\frac{12}{3} = $ _____
7. $6\frac{22}{7} = $ _____	**15.** $8\frac{16}{3} = $ _____
8. $4\frac{49}{4} = $ _____	**16.** $4\frac{9}{5} = $ _____

Basic Computation Series 2000: Understanding Fractions
SECTION 2 Least Common Denominator, Improper Fractions, and Mixed Numbers

The Decimal Number System, Decimal Numbers, and Graphing

Numbers that involve fractions can be expressed as decimal numbers as well as common fractions. A decimal number may have a whole number part as well as a fractional part, just as with common fractions, but the fractional part of a decimal number always has a "denominator" that is a power of 10.

The number system commonly in use in this country is a *place-value* system based on the number 10. That means that when writing numbers, the *value* of each digit depends on the *place* in the number where that digit is written. The places are related to powers of ten. A *decimal point* is used to separate the whole number part and the fractional part of a number. When reading a number, the decimal point is read as "and." The chart below illustrates the place-value system for decimal numbers.

10^4	10^3	10^2	10	1	decimal point	$\frac{1}{10}$	$\frac{1}{10^2}$	$\frac{1}{10^3}$	$\frac{1}{10^4}$
ten-thousands	thousands	hundreds	tens	ones	.	tenths	hundredths	thousandths	ten-thousandths

Basic Computation Series 2000: Understanding Fractions
SECTION 3 The Decimal Number System, Decimal Numbers, and Graphing

69

Example 1: Write each number in the chart in words.

	10^4	10^3	10^2	10	1	decimal point	$\frac{1}{10}$	$\frac{1}{10^2}$	$\frac{1}{10^3}$	$\frac{1}{10^4}$
a.					0	.	5			
b.					0	.	2	4		
c.					0	.	0	6	2	
d.			4	2	6	.	1	8	0	1
e.		6	5	9	0	.	4	3		
f.	9	3	1	7	2	.	6	2	5	

Solution: **a.** five tenths

b. twenty-four hundredths

c. sixty-two thousandths

d. four hundred twenty-six and one thousand eight hundred one ten-thousandths

e. six thousand five hundred ninety and forty-three hundredths

f. ninety-three thousand one hundred seventy-two and six hundred twenty-five thousandths

Notice in Example 1, that when a decimal number is less than 1, it is conventional to write a 0 to the left of the decimal point (in the ones place).

Example 2: Fill in the chart on the next page by writing the digits of each number in the proper places.

a. four hundred fifty-two and eleven thousandths

b. two thousand seventy five and six hundred seventy-four thousandths

c. twenty-seven thousand one hundred fifty-four and seventy-five hundredths

d. six hundred ninety-two and five tenths

Solution:

	10^4	10^3	10^2	10	1	decimal point	$\frac{1}{10}$	$\frac{1}{10^2}$	$\frac{1}{10^3}$	$\frac{1}{10^4}$
a.			4	5	2	.	0	1	1	
b.		2	0	7	5	.	6	7	4	
c.	2	7	1	5	4	.	7	5		
d.			6	9	2	.	5			

A *number line* is used for graphing numbers. Points on the line are marked to represent different numbers. The space between points that represent whole numbers can be divided in such a way so that fractions can be represented. For example, if the space between two whole numbers is divided into four equal parts, then each of the equal parts would represent $\frac{1}{4}$.

Example 3: Graph each of the following numbers on the number line below by making a dot on the point that represents each number. Identify each point with the number it represents and the corresponding letter.

a. A: $\frac{1}{4}$

b. B: $\frac{3}{2}$

c. C: $\frac{22}{8}$

Solution:　**a.** Make a dot on the point that is $\frac{1}{4}$ of the distance from 0 to 1 and label it A.

b. Since $\frac{3}{2} = 1\frac{1}{2}$, make a dot on the point that is $\frac{1}{2}$ the distance between 1 and 2 and label it B.

c. Since $\frac{22}{8} = 2\frac{3}{4}$, make a dot on the point that is $\frac{3}{4}$ the distance between 2 and 3 and label it C.

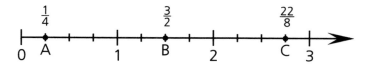

Basic Computation Series 2000: Understanding Fractions
SECTION 3　The Decimal Number System, Decimal Numbers, and Graphing

71

Example 4: Graph each of the following numbers on the number line below and label each graph.

　　a. A: 0.3

　　b. B: 1.2

　　c. C: 2.4

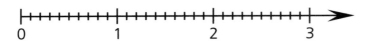

Solution: The space between whole numbers on the number line is divided into ten parts; thus, each part represents one tenth. From each whole number, count the number of spaces to the desired tenth.

In order to read a number that is graphed on a number line, first identify the largest whole number to the left of the point graphed. This is the whole number part of the number. Next, determine the number of equal parts into which the space between whole numbers has been divided. Count the spaces between the whole number and the point to determine the fractional part of the number.

Example 5: Write the number corresponding to the point marked by each letter on the graph. Write fractions in lowest terms, and fractions greater than 1 as mixed numbers in simplest form.

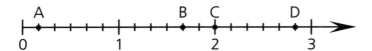

Solution: The space between whole numbers on this number line is divided into 6 equal parts; thus, each part represents $\frac{1}{6}$. Point A is located 1 space to the right of 0, and therefore represents the number $\frac{1}{6}$. Point B is located 4 spaces to the right of 1, and therefore represents $1\frac{4}{6}$. In simplest form, $1\frac{4}{6}$ is $1\frac{2}{3}$. Point C is located on the number 2. Point D is located 5 spaces to the right of 2, and therefore represents the number $2\frac{5}{6}$.

Basic Computation Series 2000: Understanding Fractions
SECTION 3 The Decimal Number System, Decimal Numbers, and Graphing

72

Example 6: State the decimal number corresponding to the point marked by each letter on the graph below.

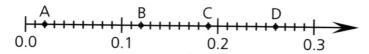

Solution: The larger divisions on the graph represent tenths (0.1, 0.2, 0.3). Since there are 10 of the smaller divisions between each of the tenths, each of the smaller divisions represents 0.01. Since point A is two spaces to the right of 0.0, point A corresponds to 0.02. Point B is two spaces to the right of 0.1, thus it corresponds to 0.12. Similarly, point C corresponds to 0.19, and point D corresponds to 0.26.

To change a common fraction to a decimal number, divide the denominator into the numerator. The quotient will be the equivalent decimal form of the number. In order to accomplish this division, place a decimal point to the right of the numerator and annex sufficient zeros to the right of the decimal point. It may take some experimentation to know exactly how many zeros will be needed to complete the division. Annex zeros until the remainder is zero or until it sets up a pattern of repeating digits. A repeating block of digits will develop whenever a remainder is repeated. The number of digits in a repeating block will be less than the divisor. A repeating block of digits is indicated with a bar placed over all the digits in the block.

Examples: $\frac{1}{9} = 0.\overline{1}$ $\frac{3}{7} = 0.\overline{428571}$ $\frac{8}{45} = 0.1\overline{7}$

When dividing a whole number into a decimal number, divide as you normally would with whole numbers, and place a decimal point in your quotient directly above the decimal point in the dividend.

Example 7: **a.** Rewrite $\frac{3}{4}$ in decimal form.

      b. Rewrite $\frac{5}{11}$ in decimal form.

Solution: **a.** Divide the denominator, 4, into the numerator, 3.

$$
\begin{array}{r}
0.75 \\
4\overline{)3.00} \\
\underline{2\ 8} \\
20 \\
\underline{20} \\
0
\end{array}
$$

Thus, the decimal form of $\frac{3}{4}$ is 0.75.

b. Divide the denominator, 11, into the numerator, 5.

$$
\begin{array}{r}
0.45 \\
11\overline{)5.00} \\
\underline{4\ 4} \\
60 \\
\underline{55} \\
5
\end{array}
$$

Basic Computation Series 2000: Understanding Fractions
SECTION 3 The Decimal Number System, Decimal Numbers, and Graphing

73

After annexing two zeros and dividing, the remainder is 5. Since this remainder is the same as the first partial dividend, 5, the division will repeat itself over and over again, and, therefore, the digits in the quotient will repeat as a block.

$$
\begin{array}{r}
0.4545 \\
11\overline{)5.0000} \\
\underline{4\,4} \\
60 \\
\underline{55} \\
50 \\
\underline{44} \\
60 \\
\underline{55} \\
5
\end{array}
$$

Thus, the decimal form of $\frac{5}{11}$ is $0.\overline{45}$.

To write a decimal fraction as a common fraction, write the digits of the decimal number as the numerator of the fraction. The denominator will be the power of ten corresponding to the number of decimal places. To reduce the fraction, divide the numerator and denominator by their greatest common factor. As an aid for reducing, it is helpful to know that 2 and 5 are each a factor the same number of times as there are zeros in the power of ten. For example, $10^4 = 2^4 \times 5^4$.

Example 8: Rewrite 0.625 as a common fraction in lowest terms.

Solution: $0.625 = \frac{625}{1000}$. In factored form, $625 = 5 \times 5 \times 5 \times 5$, or 5^4. In factored form $1,000 = 2^3 \times 5^3$. Since the GCF of 625 and 1,000 is 5^3, divide the numerator and denominator by 5^3 to reduce the fraction. Thus, $0.625 = \frac{5}{8}$.

Basic Computation Series 2000: Understanding Fractions
SECTION 3 The Decimal Number System, Decimal Numbers, and Graphing

NAME

DATE

Reading Decimal Numbers

Write each number in the chart in words. Remember, the decimal point is read as "and."

	10^4	10^3	10^2	10	1	decimal point	$\frac{1}{10}$	$1\backslash10^2$	$\frac{1}{10^3}$	$\frac{1}{10^4}$
1.					0	.	8			
2.				2	7	.	4			
3.					6	.	2	3	4	
4.			5	1	0	.	6	1		
5.				3	9	.	5	2	7	
6.		4	0	0	2	.	7			
7.	7	4	6	2	1	.	2	8		
8.				8	0	.	0	9		
9.					7	.	3	2	5	
10.			2	5	6	.	4	9		

Answers:

1. _eight tenths_

2. _____

3. _____

4. _____

5. _____

6. _____

7. _____

8. _____

9. _____

10. _____

Basic Computation Series 2000: Understanding Fractions
SECTION 3 The Decimal Number System, Decimal Numbers, and Graphing

75

Writing Decimal Numbers

Fill in the chart by writing the digits of each number in the proper places.

1. seven tenths

2. forty-two hundredths

3. five and six tenths

4. one hundred five and fifty-seven thousandths

5. two thousand eight and four tenths

6. twenty-seven and four hundred five thousandths

7. thirty-seven and twenty-one thousandths

8. four thousand fifty-two and eleven hundredths

9. fourteen and fifty-eight hundredths

10. two hundred seventeen and eighty-three thousandths

Answers:

	10^4	10^3	10^2	10	1	decimal point	$\frac{1}{10}$	$\frac{1}{10^2}$	$\frac{1}{10^3}$	$\frac{1}{10^4}$
1.					0	.	7			
2.						.				
3.						.				
4.						.				
5.						.				
6.						.				
7.						.				
8.						.				
9.						.				
10.						.				

Basic Computation Series 2000: Understanding Fractions
SECTION 3 The Decimal Number System, Decimal Numbers, and Graphing

76

Reading Decimal Numbers

Write each number in the chart in words. Remember, the decimal point is read as "and."

	10^4	10^3	10^2	10	1	decimal point	$\frac{1}{10}$	$\frac{1}{10^2}$	$\frac{1}{10^3}$	$\frac{1}{10^4}$
1.					0	.	3	5		
2.				4	2	.	7			
3.			2	0	6	.	4			
4.				8	5	.	2	1		
5.			3	1	2	.	0	6		
6.				4	3	.	0	0	5	
7.		8	2	2	0	.	1			
8.				5	9	.	8			
9.					4	.	0	3	5	
10.				9	1	.	5	7		

Answers:

1. <u>thirty-five hundredths</u>

2. _____

3. _____

4. _____

5. _____

6. _____

7. _____

8. _____

9. _____

10. _____

Basic Computation Series 2000: Understanding Fractions
SECTION 3 The Decimal Number System, Decimal Numbers, and Graphing

77

Writing Decimal Numbers

Fill in the chart by writing the digits of each number in the proper places.

1. fifty-three and two tenths

2. six hundred seven and five hundredths

3. eight and four hundred twenty-one ten-thousandths

4. sixty-six and five thousandths

5. two thousand eight hundred three and fifty-nine hundredths

6. six hundred seventy-two and four thousand three hundred forty-three ten-thousandths

7. seventy-six thousand ninety-five and two tenths

8. eight hundred sixty-one and seventy-two hundredths

9. nine and five hundred seven thousandths

10. twenty-three and eighty-four hundredths

Answers:

	10^4	10^3	10^2	10	1	decimal point	$\frac{1}{10}$	$\frac{1}{10^2}$	$\frac{1}{10^3}$	$\frac{1}{10^4}$
1.				5	3	.	2			
2.						.				
3.						.				
4.						.				
5.						.				
6.						.				
7.						.				
8.						.				
9.						.				
10.						.				

Basic Computation Series 2000: Understanding Fractions
SECTION 3 The Decimal Number System, Decimal Numbers, and Graphing

Reading Decimal Numbers

Write each number in the chart in words. Remember, the decimal point is read as "and."

	10^4	10^3	10^2	10	1	decimal point	$\frac{1}{10}$	$\frac{1}{10^2}$	$\frac{1}{10^3}$	$\frac{1}{10^4}$
1.				2	3	.	8			
2.			4	0	6	.	5	9		
3.					9	.	2	0	7	
4.				5	6	.	3	0	0	5
5.		6	2	1	8	.	6			
6.				1	7	.	0	2		
7.			2	4	3	.	1	0	9	
8.	6	7	2	0	9	.	4			
9.				6	2	.	9	1		
10.					5	.	3	7	5	

Answers:

1. _twenty-three and eight tenths_

2. _____

3. _____

4. _____

5. _____

6. _____

7. _____

8. _____

9. _____

10. _____

Basic Computation Series 2000: Understanding Fractions
SECTION 3 The Decimal Number System, Decimal Numbers, and Graphing

79

Writing Decimal Numbers

Fill in the chart by writing the digits of each number in the proper places.

1. four and twenty-nine hundredths

2. six hundred two thousandths

3. ninety-five and four hundred sixteen thousandths

4. four hundred seven and thirty-two hundredths

5. two thousand five hundred sixty-one and eight thousandths

6. seventy-five and two tenths

7. nine hundred six and forty-three hundredths

8. two thousand seventy-four and five hundredths

9. twenty-nine and thirty-two hundredths

10. sixty thousand one hundred fifty-seven and two hundred nine ten-thousandths

Answers:

	10^4	10^3	10^2	10	1	decimal point	$\frac{1}{10}$	$\frac{1}{10^2}$	$\frac{1}{10^3}$	$\frac{1}{10^4}$
1.					4	.	2	9		
2.						.				
3.						.				
4.						.				
5.						.				
6.						.				
7.						.				
8.						.				
9.						.				
10.						.				

Basic Computation Series 2000: Understanding Fractions
SECTION 3 The Decimal Number System, Decimal Numbers, and Graphing

Reading Decimal Numbers

Write each number in the chart in words. Remember, the decimal point is read as "and."

	10^4	10^3	10^2	10	1	decimal point	$\frac{1}{10}$	$\frac{1}{10^2}$	$\frac{1}{10^3}$	$\frac{1}{10^4}$
1.				4	3	.	2	6		
2.					0	.	5	7	2	
3.				2	8	.	9	0	6	
4.			4	1	7	.	2	8		
5.					0	.	5	1	2	
6.				6	7	.	4	3		
7.			2	0	5	.	3			
8.	5	6	4	3	2	.	0	5		
9.			2	7	3	.	9	2		
10.				7	8	.	7			

Answers:

1. <u>forty-three and twenty-six hundredths</u>

2. _____

3. _____

4. _____

5. _____

6. _____

7. _____

8. _____

9. _____

10. _____

Basic Computation Series 2000: Understanding Fractions
SECTION 3 The Decimal Number System, Decimal Numbers, and Graphing

81

Writing Decimal Numbers

Fill in the chart by writing the digits of each number in the proper places.

1. fifty-six hundredths

2. twenty-nine and three hundred twenty-one thousandths

3. eight hundred six and ninety-three hundredths

4. five thousand seven hundred forty-one and two hundredths

5. ninety-six and seventy-five hundredths

6. four and three tenths

7. eight hundred seventy-nine and five hundred sixty-two thousandths

8. sixty-seven and three tenths

9. fifty-seven hundredths

10. ninety-three thousand four hundred eighteen and twenty-seven hundredths

Answers:

	10^4	10^3	10^2	10	1	decimal point	$\frac{1}{10}$	$\frac{1}{10^2}$	$\frac{1}{10^3}$	$\frac{1}{10^4}$
1.					0	.	5	6		
2.						.				
3.						.				
4.						.				
5.						.				
6.						.				
7.						.				
8.						.				
9.						.				
10.						.				

Basic Computation Series 2000: Understanding Fractions
SECTION 3 The Decimal Number System, Decimal Numbers, and Graphing

Reading Decimal Numbers

Write each number in the chart in words. Remember, the decimal point is read as "and."

	10^4	10^3	10^2	10	1	decimal point	$\frac{1}{10}$	$\frac{1}{10^2}$	$\frac{1}{10^3}$	$\frac{1}{10^4}$
1.				2	6	.	3			
2.					0	.	9	5		
3.		6	0	7	1	.	2	9		
4.			4	3	5	.	6	3	1	
5.	4	3	2	1	7	.	4			
6.			6	0	6	.	7	0	7	
7.			5	3	1	.	2	1	5	
8.				3	9	.	5			
9.				5	8	.	2			
10.			9	4	0	.	7	2		

Answers:

1. twenty-six and three tenths

2. _____

3. _____

4. _____

5. _____

6. _____

7. _____

8. _____

9. _____

10. _____

Basic Computation Series 2000: Understanding Fractions
SECTION 3 The Decimal Number System, Decimal Numbers, and Graphing

83

Writing Decimal Numbers

Fill in the chart by writing the digits of each number in the proper places.

1. ninety-two and five tenths

2. six and seven hundred fourteen thousandths

3. eighty and thirty-two hundredths

4. nine and two tenths

5. ninety-five hundredths

6. eight hundred thirty-two and sixty-seven hundredths

7. forty-three thousand two hundred one and two tenths

8. five hundred seventy-five and thirty-one hundredths

9. seven thousand five ten thousandths

10. sixty-nine and fifty-two hundredths

Answers:

	10^4	10^3	10^2	10	1	decimal point	$\frac{1}{10}$	$\frac{1}{10^2}$	$\frac{1}{10^3}$	$\frac{1}{10^4}$
1.				9	2	.	5			
2.						.				
3.						.				
4.						.				
5.						.				
6.						.				
7.						.				
8.						.				
9.						.				
10.						.				

84

Basic Computation Series 2000: Understanding Fractions
SECTION 3 The Decimal Number System, Decimal Numbers, and Graphing

Graphing on a Number Line

Graph the given numbers on the number line. Write the letter corresponding to the number above its graph.

1.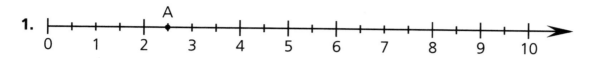

A: $2\frac{1}{2}$ **B:** 3   **C:** $\frac{8}{2}$ **D:** $\frac{7}{2}$ **E:** $6\frac{1}{2}$

F: $\frac{25}{5}$ **G:** $\frac{17}{2}$ **H:** $\frac{57}{6}$ **I:** $\frac{11}{2}$ **J:** $\frac{12}{2}$

2.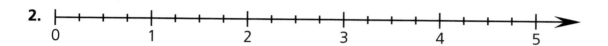

A: $\frac{17}{4}$ **B:** $\frac{3}{4}$ **C:** $\frac{14}{4}$ **D:** $\frac{15}{4}$ **E:** $\frac{20}{8}$

F: $1\frac{3}{4}$ **G:** $\frac{9}{2}$ **H:** $\frac{3}{2}$ **I:** $\frac{18}{8}$ **J:** $\frac{38}{8}$

3.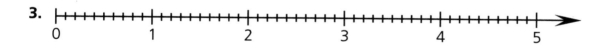

A: 1.1   **B:** 3.4   **C:** 1.7   **D:** 0.5   **E:** 2.9

F: 2.3   **G:** 2.8   **H:** 0.3   **I:** 3.8   **J:** 4.4

4.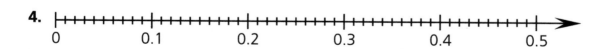

A: 0.02   **B:** 0.13   **C:** 0.28   **D:** 0.09   **E:** 0.25

F: 0.06   **G:** 0.36   **H:** 0.19   **I:** 0.34   **J:** 0.17

Basic Computation Series 2000: Understanding Fractions
SECTION 3 The Decimal Number System, Decimal Numbers, and Graphing

85

Reading Number Line Graphs

Write the number corresponding to the point marked by each letter on the graph. Write fractions in lowest terms, and fractions greater than 1 as mixed numbers in simplest form.

1.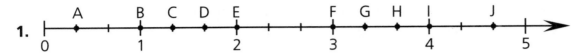

A: $\dfrac{1}{3}$ B: _____   C: _____   D: _____   E: _____

F: _____   G: _____   H: _____   I: _____   J: _____

Write the decimal number corresponding to the point marked by each letter on the graph.

2.

A: _0.02_   B: _____   C: _____   D: _____   E: _____

F: _____   G: _____   H: _____   I: _____   J: _____

86

Basic Computation Series 2000: Understanding Fractions
SECTION 3 The Decimal Number System, Decimal Numbers, and Graphing

Graphing on a Number Line

Graph the given numbers on the number line. Write the letter corresponding to the number above its graph.

1.

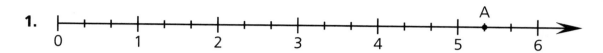

A: $\frac{16}{3}$ **B:** $\frac{11}{3}$ **C:** $\frac{6}{3}$ **D:** $1\frac{2}{3}$ **E:** $\frac{17}{3}$

F: $\frac{18}{6}$ **G:** $\frac{8}{6}$ **H:** $\frac{40}{12}$ **I:** $\frac{16}{6}$ **J:** $\frac{60}{15}$

2.

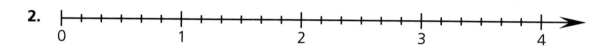

A: $\frac{16}{6}$ **B:** $\frac{24}{12}$ **C:** $\frac{5}{6}$ **D:** $2\frac{1}{2}$ **E:** $3\frac{2}{3}$

F: $2\frac{1}{3}$ **G:** $\frac{8}{6}$ **H:** $\frac{1}{3}$ **I:** $\frac{1}{2}$ **J:** $\frac{20}{6}$

3.

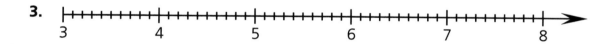

A: 4   **B:** 3.2   **C:** 4.5   **D:** 6.8   **E:** 3.9

F: 7.3   **G:** 7   **H:** 5.7   **I:** 3.7   **J:** 6.1

4.

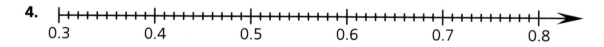

A: 0.37   **B:** 0.61   **C:** 0.45   **D:** 0.5   **E:** 0.58

F: 0.39   **G:** 0.42   **H:** 0.77   **I:** 0.7   **J:** 0.66

Basic Computation Series 2000: Understanding Fractions
SECTION 3 The Decimal Number System, Decimal Numbers, and Graphing

87

Reading Number Line Graphs

Write the number corresponding to the point marked by each letter on the graph. Write fractions in lowest terms, and fractions greater than 1 as mixed numbers in simplest form.

1.

A: $\frac{3}{5}$ B: _____   C: _____   D: _____   E: _____

F: _____   G: _____   H: _____   I: _____   J: _____

Write the decimal number corresponding to the point marked by each letter on the graph.

2.

A: _0.002_   B: _____   C: _____   D: _____   E: _____

F: _____   G: _____   H: _____   I: _____   J: _____

Basic Computation Series 2000: Understanding Fractions
SECTION 3 The Decimal Number System, Decimal Numbers, and Graphing

Graphing on a Number Line

Graph the given numbers on the number line. Write the letter corresponding to the number above its graph.

1.

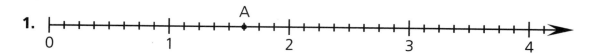

A: $\frac{13}{8}$ **B:** $\frac{5}{4}$ **C:** $\frac{1}{4}$ **D:** $\frac{29}{8}$ **E:** $\frac{7}{2}$

F: $\frac{3}{4}$ **G:** $1\frac{3}{8}$ **H:** $\frac{23}{8}$ **I:** $3\frac{1}{8}$ **J:** $1\frac{1}{2}$

2.

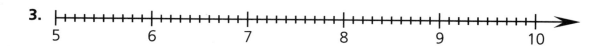

A: 4   **B:** $\frac{21}{10}$ **C:** $3\frac{1}{2}$ **D:** $3\frac{4}{5}$ **E:** $4\frac{4}{5}$

F: $\frac{21}{5}$ **G:** $\frac{54}{10}$ **H:** $6\frac{3}{10}$ **I:** $4\frac{1}{2}$ **J:** $3\frac{1}{10}$

3.

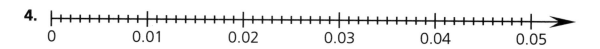

A: 6   **B:** 7.7   **C:** 5.2   **D:** 8.1   **E:** 9.9

F: 8.9   **G:** 5.8   **H:** 6.9   **I:** 8.3   **J:** 7.5

4.

A: 0.002   **B:** 0.01   **C:** 0.023   **D:** 0.007   **E:** 0.015

F: 0.045   **G:** 0.019   **H:** 0.027   **I:** 0.049   **J:** 0.036

Basic Computation Series 2000: Understanding Fractions
SECTION 3 The Decimal Number System, Decimal Numbers, and Graphing

89

Reading Number Line Graphs

Write the number corresponding to the point marked by each letter on the graph. Write fractions in lowest terms, and fractions greater than 1 as mixed numbers in simplest form.

1.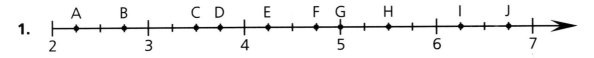

A: $2\frac{1}{4}$ B: _____   C: _____   D: _____   E: _____

F: _____   G: _____   H: _____   I: _____   J: _____

Write the decimal number corresponding to the point marked by each letter on the graph.

2.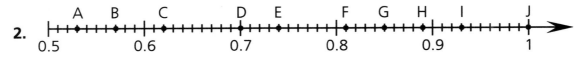

A: 0.53 B: _____   C: _____   D: _____   E: _____

F: _____   G: _____   H: _____   I: _____   J: _____

Basic Computation Series 2000: Understanding Fractions
SECTION 3 The Decimal Number System, Decimal Numbers, and Graphing

Graphing on a Number Line

Graph the given numbers on the number line. Write the letter corresponding to the number above its graph.

1.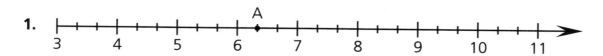

A: $\frac{38}{6}$ B: $4\frac{1}{3}$ C: $\frac{68}{12}$ D: $\frac{11}{3}$ E: $6\frac{2}{3}$

F: $\frac{44}{6}$ G: $\frac{24}{6}$ H: $\frac{25}{3}$ I: $\frac{56}{6}$ J: $\frac{32}{6}$

2.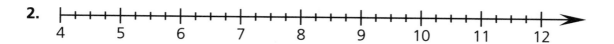

A: $6\frac{1}{2}$ B: $\frac{58}{8}$ C: $\frac{18}{4}$ D: $\frac{27}{4}$ E: $\frac{35}{4}$

F: $10\frac{3}{4}$ G: $\frac{46}{8}$ H: $\frac{33}{4}$ I: $\frac{17}{2}$ J: $\frac{11}{2}$

3.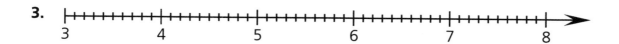

A: 5.2   B: 3.2   C: 4.5   D: 5.8   E: 7.2

F: 3.5   G: 6.4   H: 7.3   I: 6.9   J: 3.7

4.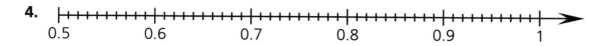

A: 0.51   B: 0.73   C: 0.93   D: 0.56   E: 0.98

F: 0.85   G: 0.77   H: 0.62   I: 0.88   J: 0.65

Basic Computation Series 2000: Understanding Fractions
SECTION 3 The Decimal Number System, Decimal Numbers, and Graphing

91

Reading Number Line Graphs

Write the number corresponding to the point marked by each letter on the graph. Write fractions in lowest terms, and fractions greater than 1 as mixed numbers in simplest form.

1.

A: $4\frac{3}{8}$ B: _____   C: _____   D: _____   E: _____

F: _____   G: _____   H: _____   I: _____   J: _____

Write the decimal number corresponding to the point marked by each letter on the graph.

2.

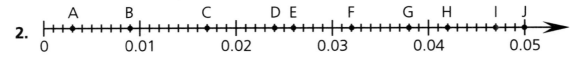

A: 0.003 B: _____   C: _____   D: _____   E: _____

F: _____   G: _____   H: _____   I: _____   J: _____

Graphing on a Number Line

Graph the given numbers on the number line. Write the letter corresponding to the number above its graph.

1.

A

0 1 2 3 4 5 6 7

A: $4\frac{2}{3}$ **B:** $\frac{4}{3}$ **C:** $\frac{16}{3}$ **D:** $\frac{1}{3}$ **E:** $3\frac{1}{3}$

F: $\frac{40}{15}$ **G:** $\frac{28}{12}$ **H:** $\frac{8}{6}$ **I:** $\frac{39}{9}$ **J:** $\frac{40}{6}$

2.

3 4 5 6 7 8 9 10 11

A: $\frac{15}{4}$ **B:** $\frac{23}{4}$ **C:** $6\frac{1}{2}$ **D:** $8\frac{3}{4}$ **E:** 10

F: $\frac{15}{2}$ **G:** $\frac{74}{8}$ **H:** $\frac{64}{16}$ **I:** $9\frac{1}{4}$ **J:** $\frac{31}{4}$

3.

0 1 2 3 4 5

A: 0.5   **B:** 4.2   **C:** 1.3   **D:** 2.0   **E:** 4.6

F: 3.8   **G:** 0.2   **H:** 2.7   **I:** 4.4   **J:** 5.1

4.

0.5 0.6 0.7 0.8 0.9 1.0

A: 0.74   **B:** 0.5   **C:** 0.80   **D:** 0.57   **E:** 0.96

F: 0.82   **G:** 0.71   **H:** 0.67   **I:** 0.92   **J:** 0.63

Basic Computation Series 2000: Understanding Fractions
SECTION 3 The Decimal Number System, Decimal Numbers, and Graphing

93

Reading Number Line Graphs

Write the number corresponding to the point marked by each letter on the graph. Write fractions in lowest terms, and fractions greater than 1 as mixed numbers in simplest form.

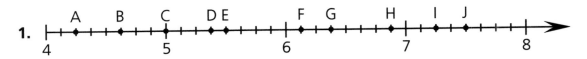

1.

A: $4\frac{1}{4}$ B: _____   C: _____   D: _____   E: _____

F: _____   G: _____   H: _____   I: _____   J: _____

Write the decimal number corresponding to the point marked by each letter on the graph.

2.

A: 0.002   B: _____   C: _____   D: _____   E: _____

F: _____   G: _____   H: _____   I: _____   J: _____

Basic Computation Series 2000: Understanding Fractions
SECTION 3 The Decimal Number System, Decimal Numbers, and Graphing

94

Converting Fractions to Decimals

Write each fraction in decimal form.

1. $\frac{1}{2} =$ ___0.5___	**11.** $\frac{7}{18} =$ _____
2. $\frac{1}{4} =$ _____	**12.** $\frac{2}{7} =$ _____
3. $\frac{5}{12} =$ _____	**13.** $\frac{5}{32} =$ _____
4. $\frac{4}{15} =$ _____	**14.** $\frac{1}{3} =$ _____
5. $\frac{7}{20} =$ _____	**15.** $\frac{7}{22} =$ _____
6. $\frac{5}{11} =$ _____	**16.** $\frac{1}{9} =$ _____
7. $\frac{3}{8} =$ _____	**17.** $\frac{2}{5} =$ _____
8. $\frac{3}{16} =$ _____	**18.** $\frac{3}{4} =$ _____
9. $\frac{7}{24} =$ _____	**19.** $\frac{4}{5} =$ _____
10. $\frac{3}{10} =$ _____	**20.** $\frac{7}{10} =$ _____

Basic Computation Series 2000: Understanding Fractions
SECTION 3 The Decimal Number System, Decimal Numbers, and Graphing

95

Converting Decimals to Fractions

Write each decimal number as a fraction in lowest terms.

1. $0.2 = \dfrac{1}{5}$	**11.** $0.65 = $ _____
2. $0.9 = $ _____	**12.** $0.25 = $ _____
3. $0.375 = $ _____	**13.** $0.16 = $ _____
4. $0.8 = $ _____	**14.** $0.3 = $ _____
5. $0.42 = $ _____	**15.** $0.4 = $ _____
6. $0.5 = $ _____	**16.** $0.305 = $ _____
7. $0.15625 = $ _____	**17.** $0.35 = $ _____
8. $0.43 = $ _____	**18.** $0.115 = $ _____
9. $0.1875 = $ _____	**19.** $0.75 = $ _____
10. $0.7 = $ _____	**20.** $0.12 = $ _____

96

Basic Computation Series 2000: Understanding Fractions
SECTION 3 The Decimal Number System, Decimal Numbers, and Graphing

Converting Fractions to Decimals

Write each fraction in decimal form.

1. $\frac{1}{10}$ = _____ _O.1_ _____	**11.** $\frac{1}{2}$ = _____
2. $\frac{7}{9}$ = _____	**12.** $\frac{3}{25}$ = _____
3. $\frac{5}{6}$ = _____	**13.** $\frac{1}{8}$ = _____
4. $\frac{11}{32}$ = _____	**14.** $\frac{5}{24}$ = _____
5. $\frac{2}{3}$ = _____	**15.** $\frac{3}{4}$ = _____
6. $\frac{1}{7}$ = _____	**16.** $\frac{7}{15}$ = _____
7. $\frac{7}{16}$ = _____	**17.** $\frac{9}{20}$ = _____
8. $\frac{3}{5}$ = _____	**18.** $\frac{5}{7}$ = _____
9. $\frac{4}{9}$ = _____	**19.** $\frac{3}{22}$ = _____
10. $\frac{1}{11}$ = _____	**20.** $\frac{1}{18}$ = _____

Basic Computation Series 2000: Understanding Fractions
SECTION 3 The Decimal Number System, Decimal Numbers, and Graphing

97

Converting Decimals to Fractions

Write each decimal number as a fraction in lowest terms.

1. $0.75 = \dfrac{3}{4}$	**11.** $0.45 = \underline{\hspace{2em}}$
2. $0.6 = \underline{\hspace{2em}}$	**12.** $0.14 = \underline{\hspace{2em}}$
3. $0.125 = \underline{\hspace{2em}}$	**13.** $0.12 = \underline{\hspace{2em}}$
4. $0.1 = \underline{\hspace{2em}}$	**14.** $0.67 = \underline{\hspace{2em}}$
5. $0.15 = \underline{\hspace{2em}}$	**15.** $0.95 = \underline{\hspace{2em}}$
6. $0.5 = \underline{\hspace{2em}}$	**16.** $0.46 = \underline{\hspace{2em}}$
7. $0.725 = \underline{\hspace{2em}}$	**17.** $0.28 = \underline{\hspace{2em}}$
8. $0.84 = \underline{\hspace{2em}}$	**18.** $0.9 = \underline{\hspace{2em}}$
9. $0.4375 = \underline{\hspace{2em}}$	**19.** $0.875 = \underline{\hspace{2em}}$
10. $0.32 = \underline{\hspace{2em}}$	**20.** $0.25 = \underline{\hspace{2em}}$

Basic Computation Series 2000: Understanding Fractions
SECTION 3 The Decimal Number System, Decimal Numbers, and Graphing

98

Converting Fractions to Decimals

Write each fraction in decimal form.

1. $\frac{3}{4}$ = _____0.75_____	**11.** $\frac{5}{22}$ = _____
2. $\frac{7}{25}$ = _____	**12.** $\frac{1}{5}$ = _____
3. $\frac{1}{2}$ = _____	**13.** $\frac{5}{24}$ = _____
4. $\frac{5}{9}$ = _____	**14.** $\frac{9}{10}$ = _____
5. $\frac{9}{20}$ = _____	**15.** $\frac{4}{7}$ = _____
6. $\frac{3}{11}$ = _____	**16.** $\frac{7}{12}$ = _____
7. $\frac{5}{36}$ = _____	**17.** $\frac{7}{8}$ = _____
8. $\frac{7}{32}$ = _____	**18.** $\frac{1}{15}$ = _____
9. $\frac{5}{27}$ = _____	**19.** $\frac{7}{33}$ = _____
10. $\frac{1}{3}$ = _____	**20.** $\frac{7}{30}$ = _____

Basic Computation Series 2000: Understanding Fractions
SECTION 3 The Decimal Number System, Decimal Numbers, and Graphing

99

Converting Decimals to Fractions

Write each decimal number as a fraction in lowest terms.

1. 0.25 = $\frac{1}{4}$	**11.** 0.05 = _____
2. 0.8 = _____	**12.** 0.215 = _____
3. 0.7 = _____	**13.** 0.66 = _____
4. 0.12 = _____	**14.** 0.35 = _____
5. 0.24 = _____	**15.** 0.135 = _____
6. 0.1875 = _____	**16.** 0.18 = _____
7. 0.91 = _____	**17.** 0.615 = _____
8. 0.5 = _____	**18.** 0.04 = _____
9. 0.62 = _____	**19.** 0.0375 = _____
10. 0.625 = _____	**20.** 0.01 = _____

Basic Computation Series 2000: Understanding Fractions
SECTION 3 The Decimal Number System, Decimal Numbers, and Graphing

NAME _____ DATE _____

Converting Fractions to Decimals

Write each fraction in decimal form.

1. $\frac{4}{5}$ = _____ 0.8 _____	**11.** $\frac{7}{10}$ = _____
2. $\frac{3}{7}$ = _____	**12.** $\frac{5}{8}$ = _____
3. $\frac{3}{25}$ = _____	**13.** $\frac{2}{9}$ = _____
4. $\frac{1}{6}$ = _____	**14.** $\frac{7}{20}$ = _____
5. $\frac{1}{4}$ = _____	**15.** $\frac{1}{2}$ = _____
6. $\frac{7}{12}$ = _____	**16.** $\frac{9}{32}$ = _____
7. $\frac{8}{9}$ = _____	**17.** $\frac{10}{11}$ = _____
8. $\frac{3}{16}$ = _____	**18.** $\frac{2}{3}$ = _____
9. $\frac{5}{33}$ = _____	**19.** $\frac{11}{15}$ = _____
10. $\frac{5}{18}$ = _____	**20.** $\frac{6}{7}$ = _____

Basic Computation Series 2000: Understanding Fractions
SECTION 3 The Decimal Number System, Decimal Numbers, and Graphing

101

NAME _____   DATE _____

Converting Decimals to Fractions

Write each decimal number as a fraction in lowest terms.

1. $0.9 = \frac{9}{10}$	**11.** $0.08 = $ _____
2. $0.5 = $ _____	**12.** $0.21875 = $ _____
3. $0.38 = $ _____	**13.** $0.85 = $ _____
4. $0.035 = $ _____	**14.** $0.36 = $ _____
5. $0.75 = $ _____	**15.** $0.375 = $ _____
6. $0.64 = $ _____	**16.** $0.3 = $ _____
7. $0.45 = $ _____	**17.** $0.09 = $ _____
8. $0.88 = $ _____	**18.** $0.095 = $ _____
9. $0.2 = $ _____	**19.** $0.87 = $ _____
10. $0.075 = $ _____	**20.** $0.96 = $ _____

Copyright © Dale Seymour Publications®

102

Basic Computation Series 2000: Understanding Fractions
SECTION 3 The Decimal Number System, Decimal Numbers, and Graphing

NAME _____   DATE _____

Converting Fractions to Decimals

Write each fraction in decimal form.

1. $\frac{1}{5} = $ _____0.2_____

2. $\frac{5}{12} = $ _____

3. $\frac{7}{9} = $ _____

4. $\frac{9}{32} = $ _____

5. $\frac{3}{4} = $ _____

6. $\frac{8}{9} = $ _____

7. $\frac{1}{16} = $ _____

8. $\frac{3}{7} = $ _____

9. $\frac{2}{3} = $ _____

10. $\frac{9}{16} = $ _____

11. $\frac{3}{10} = $ _____

12. $\frac{5}{7} = $ _____

13. $\frac{1}{2} = $ _____

14. $\frac{5}{8} = $ _____

15. $\frac{3}{5} = $ _____

16. $\frac{7}{32} = $ _____

17. $\frac{11}{24} = $ _____

18. $\frac{3}{20} = $ _____

19. $\frac{6}{25} = $ _____

20. $\frac{7}{22} = $ _____

Basic Computation Series 2000: Understanding Fractions
SECTION 3 The Decimal Number System, Decimal Numbers, and Graphing

Converting Decimals to Fractions

Write each decimal number as a fraction in lowest terms.

1. $0.1 = \dfrac{1}{10}$

2. $0.67 = $ _____

3. $0.84 = $ _____

4. $0.25 = $ _____

5. $0.01 = $ _____

6. $0.5 = $ _____

7. $0.625 = $ _____

8. $0.33 = $ _____

9. $0.4375 = $ _____

10. $0.36 = $ _____

11. $0.14 = $ _____

12. $0.025 = $ _____

13. $0.3 = $ _____

14. $0.125 = $ _____

15. $0.45 = $ _____

16. $0.09 = $ _____

17. $0.1875 = $ _____

18. $0.6 = $ _____

19. $0.305 = $ _____

20. $0.75 = $ _____

Basic Computation Series 2000: Understanding Fractions
SECTION 3 The Decimal Number System, Decimal Numbers, and Graphing

104

Answers to Exercises

PAGE 6

1. 3, 5, $\frac{3}{5}$ **2.** 1, 6, $\frac{1}{6}$ **3.** 5, 8, $\frac{5}{8}$ **4.** 3, 7, $\frac{3}{7}$ **5.** 1, 8, $\frac{1}{8}$ **6.** 3, 8, $\frac{3}{8}$
7. 2, 9, $\frac{2}{9}$ **8.** 7, 8, $\frac{7}{8}$ **9.** 6, 7, $\frac{6}{7}$ **10.** 5, 9, $\frac{5}{9}$ **11.** $\frac{1}{2}$ **12.** $\frac{4}{5}$ **13.** $\frac{3}{4}$
14. $\frac{3}{5}$ **15.** $\frac{3}{6}$ or $\frac{1}{2}$ **16.** $\frac{2}{5}$ **17.** $\frac{1}{5}$ **18.** $\frac{6}{10}$ or $\frac{3}{5}$ **19.** $\frac{3}{9}$ or $\frac{1}{3}$ **20.** $\frac{5}{12}$

PAGE 7

1. $\frac{1}{3}$ **2.** $\frac{4}{9}$ **3.** $\frac{5}{8}$ **4.** $\frac{7}{8}$ **5.** $\frac{3}{4}$ **6.** $\frac{11}{16}$ **7.** $\frac{2}{9}$ **8.** $\frac{5}{12}$ **9.** $\frac{7}{12}$
10. $\frac{14}{30}$ or $\frac{7}{15}$ **11.** $\frac{1}{4}$ **12.** $\frac{2}{5}$ or $\frac{10}{25}$ **13.** $\frac{1}{2}$ or $\frac{5}{10}$ **14.** 40 **15.** 50
16. 3

PAGE 8

1. 2, 5, $\frac{2}{5}$ **2.** 5, 6, $\frac{5}{6}$ **3.** 5, 9, $\frac{5}{9}$ **4.** 3, 4, $\frac{3}{4}$ **5.** 7, 10, $\frac{7}{10}$
6. 2, 7, $\frac{2}{7}$ **7.** 1, 3, $\frac{1}{3}$ **8.** 5, 8, $\frac{5}{8}$ **9.** 5, 7, $\frac{5}{7}$ **10.** 1, 9, $\frac{1}{9}$ **11.** $\frac{6}{7}$
12. $\frac{3}{8}$ **13.** $\frac{4}{9}$ **14.** $\frac{5}{7}$ **15.** $\frac{3}{10}$ **16.** $\frac{8}{15}$ **17.** $\frac{3}{16}$ **18.** $\frac{5}{6}$ **19.** $\frac{11}{12}$
20. $\frac{4}{11}$

PAGE 9

1. $\frac{5}{10}$ or $\frac{1}{2}$ **2.** $\frac{2}{7}$ **3.** $\frac{4}{15}$ **4.** $\frac{1}{33}$ **5.** $\frac{12}{25}$ **6.** $\frac{40}{100}$ or $\frac{2}{5}$ **7.** $\frac{2}{2}$ or 1
8. $\frac{2}{4}$ or $\frac{1}{2}$ **9.** $\frac{3}{8}$ **10.** $\frac{3}{8}$ **11.** $\frac{1}{2}$ **12.** $\frac{1}{20}$ or $\frac{5}{100}$ **13.** $\frac{1}{5}$ **14.** 75
15. 10 **16.** 4

PAGE 10

1. 4, 7, $\frac{4}{7}$ **2.** 3, 4, $\frac{3}{4}$ **3.** 6, 7, $\frac{6}{7}$ **4.** 5, 8, $\frac{5}{8}$ **5.** 3, 10, $\frac{3}{10}$
6. 3, 8, $\frac{3}{8}$ **7.** 7, 10, $\frac{7}{10}$ **8.** 7, 8, $\frac{7}{8}$ **9.** 2, 9, $\frac{2}{9}$ **10.** 3, 5, $\frac{3}{5}$
11. $\frac{3}{8}$ **12.** $\frac{3}{6}$ or $\frac{1}{2}$ **13.** $\frac{2}{3}$ **14.** $\frac{9}{16}$ **15.** $\frac{7}{9}$ **16.** $\frac{3}{10}$ **17.** $\frac{6}{16}$ or $\frac{3}{8}$
18. $\frac{3}{7}$ **19.** $\frac{8}{9}$ **20.** $\frac{10}{13}$

PAGE 11

1. $\frac{1}{4}$ **2.** $\frac{2}{3}$ **3.** $\frac{1}{6}$ **4.** $\frac{2}{5}$ **5.** $\frac{1}{3}$ **6.** $\frac{1}{2}$ **7.** $\frac{3}{8}$ **8.** $\frac{5}{6}$ **9.** $\frac{3}{4}$ **10.** $\frac{7}{8}$
11. $\frac{1}{10}$ **12.** $\frac{1}{10}$ or $\frac{50}{500}$ **13.** $\frac{1}{5}$ or $\frac{5}{25}$ **14.** 50 **15.** 20 **16.** 4

PAGE 12

1. 7, 8, $\frac{7}{8}$ **2.** 2, 7, $\frac{2}{7}$ **3.** 5, 6, $\frac{5}{6}$ **4.** 0, 10, 0 **5.** 5, 8, $\frac{5}{8}$ **6.** 2, 3, $\frac{2}{3}$
7. 5, 9, $\frac{5}{9}$ **8.** 9, 10, $\frac{9}{10}$ **9.** 5, 7, $\frac{5}{7}$ **10.** 2, 9, $\frac{2}{9}$ **11.** $\frac{1}{2}$ **12.** $\frac{3}{5}$
13. $\frac{7}{8}$ **14.** $\frac{1}{4}$ **15.** $\frac{3}{4}$ **16.** $\frac{5}{10}$ or $\frac{1}{2}$ **17.** $\frac{3}{8}$ **18.** $\frac{3}{7}$ **19.** $\frac{4}{9}$ **20.** $\frac{10}{13}$

PAGE 13

1. $\frac{1}{4}$ **2.** $\frac{1}{2}$ **3.** $\frac{3}{4}$ **4.** $\frac{3}{16}$ **5.** $\frac{9}{16}$ **6.** $\frac{12}{16}$ or $\frac{3}{4}$ **7.** $\frac{4}{9}$ **8.** $\frac{5}{9}$ **9.** $\frac{4}{9}$
10. $\frac{11}{16}$ **11.** $\frac{1}{5}$ **12.** $\frac{1}{50}$ **13.** $\frac{1}{2}$ **14.** 25 **15.** 60 **16.** 2

PAGE 14

1. 3, 4, $\frac{3}{4}$ **2.** 3, 8, $\frac{3}{8}$ **3.** 9, 10, $\frac{9}{10}$ **4.** 4, 7, $\frac{4}{7}$ **5.** 4, 9, $\frac{4}{9}$
6. 2, 3, $\frac{2}{3}$ **7.** 7, 8, $\frac{7}{8}$ **8.** 3, 10, $\frac{3}{10}$ **9.** 5, 8, $\frac{5}{8}$ **10.** 3, 5, $\frac{3}{5}$
11. $\frac{8}{10}$ or $\frac{4}{5}$ **12.** $\frac{9}{16}$ **13.** $\frac{3}{4}$ **14.** $\frac{5}{8}$ **15.** $\frac{3}{16}$ **16.** $\frac{3}{11}$ **17.** $\frac{8}{9}$
18. $\frac{4}{6}$ or $\frac{2}{3}$ **19.** $\frac{5}{12}$ **20.** $\frac{7}{13}$

PAGE 15

1. $\frac{5}{8}$ **2.** $\frac{1}{4}$ **3.** $\frac{3}{4}$ **4.** $\frac{1}{2}$ **5.** $\frac{9}{16}$ **6.** $\frac{2}{8}$ or $\frac{1}{4}$ **7.** $\frac{1}{6}$ **8.** $\frac{2}{5}$ **9.** $\frac{6}{16}$ or $\frac{3}{8}$
10. $\frac{1}{2}$ **11.** $\frac{1}{20}$ **12.** $\frac{3}{4}$ **13.** $\frac{1}{5}$ **14.** 10 **15.** 25 **16.** 3

PAGE 16

1. $\frac{2}{4}, \frac{3}{6}, \frac{4}{8}, \frac{5}{10}, \frac{6}{12}$ **2.** $\frac{2}{6}, \frac{3}{9}, \frac{4}{12}, \frac{5}{15}, \frac{6}{18}$ **3.** $\frac{4}{6}, \frac{6}{9}, \frac{8}{12}, \frac{10}{15}, \frac{12}{18}$
4. $\frac{2}{8}, \frac{3}{12}, \frac{4}{16}, \frac{5}{20}, \frac{6}{24}$ **5.** $\frac{6}{8}, \frac{9}{12}, \frac{12}{16}, \frac{15}{20}, \frac{18}{24}$ **6.** $\frac{2}{10}, \frac{3}{15}, \frac{4}{20}, \frac{5}{25}, \frac{6}{30}$
7. $\frac{4}{10}, \frac{6}{15}, \frac{8}{20}, \frac{10}{25}, \frac{12}{30}$ **8.** $\frac{6}{10}, \frac{9}{15}, \frac{12}{20}, \frac{15}{25}, \frac{18}{30}$ **9.** $\frac{8}{10}, \frac{12}{15}, \frac{16}{20}, \frac{20}{25}, \frac{24}{30}$
10. $\frac{2}{12}, \frac{3}{18}, \frac{4}{24}, \frac{5}{30}, \frac{6}{36}$ (Note: There are other answers possible for #1–10.) **11.** 2 **12.** 4 **13.** 3 **14.** 5 **15.** 6 **16.** 12 **17.** 5 **18.** 5
19. 4 **20.** 12 **21.** 3 **22.** 3 **23.** 15 **24.** 8 **25.** 2 **26.** 4 **27.** 4
28. 8 **29.** 9 **30.** 3

PAGE 17

1. $\frac{1}{3}$ **2.** $\frac{2}{3}$ **3.** $\frac{1}{6}$ **4.** $\frac{2}{3}$ **5.** $\frac{1}{2}$ **6.** $\frac{3}{4}$ **7.** $\frac{1}{5}$ **8.** $\frac{1}{4}$ **9.** $\frac{1}{7}$ **10.** $\frac{1}{2}$
11. $\frac{2}{3}$ **12.** $\frac{3}{5}$ **13.** $\frac{4}{5}$ **14.** $\frac{1}{5}$ **15.** $\frac{2}{3}$ **16.** $\frac{1}{8}$ **17.** $\frac{1}{5}$ **18.** $\frac{1}{4}$ **19.** $\frac{7}{16}$
20. $\frac{1}{4}$

PAGE 18

1. $\frac{6}{8}, \frac{9}{12}, \frac{12}{16}, \frac{15}{20}, \frac{18}{24}$ **2.** $\frac{4}{10}, \frac{6}{15}, \frac{8}{20}, \frac{10}{25}, \frac{12}{30}$ **3.** $\frac{10}{12}, \frac{15}{18}, \frac{20}{24}, \frac{25}{30}, \frac{30}{36}$
4. $\frac{6}{14}, \frac{9}{21}, \frac{12}{28}, \frac{15}{35}, \frac{18}{42}$ **5.** $\frac{6}{16}, \frac{9}{24}, \frac{12}{32}, \frac{15}{40}, \frac{18}{48}$ **6.** $\frac{2}{6}, \frac{3}{9}, \frac{4}{12}, \frac{5}{15}, \frac{6}{18}$
7. $\frac{10}{16}, \frac{15}{24}, \frac{20}{32}, \frac{25}{40}, \frac{30}{48}$ **8.** $\frac{14}{18}, \frac{21}{27}, \frac{28}{36}, \frac{35}{45}, \frac{42}{54}$ **9.** $\frac{6}{10}, \frac{9}{15}, \frac{12}{20}, \frac{15}{25}, \frac{18}{30}$
10. $\frac{16}{18}, \frac{24}{27}, \frac{32}{36}, \frac{40}{45}, \frac{48}{54}$ (Note: There are other answers possible for #1–10.) **11.** 5 **12.** 10 **13.** 5 **14.** 10 **15.** 14 **16.** 9 **17.** 10
18. 2 **19.** 8 **20.** 27 **21.** 4 **22.** 6 **23.** 30 **24.** 12 **25.** 8
26. 15 **27.** 5 **28.** 6 **29.** 18 **30.** 6

PAGE 19

1. $\frac{1}{2}$ **2.** $\frac{2}{3}$ **3.** $\frac{2}{3}$ **4.** $\frac{3}{5}$ **5.** $\frac{1}{4}$ **6.** $\frac{6}{7}$ **7.** $\frac{1}{3}$ **8.** $\frac{5}{6}$ **9.** $\frac{7}{10}$ **10.** $\frac{2}{3}$
11. $\frac{5}{9}$ **12.** $\frac{2}{3}$ **13.** $\frac{4}{7}$ **14.** $\frac{5}{7}$ **15.** $\frac{3}{5}$ **16.** $\frac{9}{10}$ **17.** $\frac{3}{5}$ **18.** $\frac{1}{3}$ **19.** $\frac{7}{12}$
20. $\frac{7}{8}$

PAGE 20

1. $\frac{10}{21}, \frac{15}{28}, \frac{20}{35}, \frac{25}{42}, \frac{30}{?}$ **2.** $\frac{2}{4}, \frac{3}{6}, \frac{4}{8}, \frac{5}{10}, \frac{6}{12}$ **3.** $\frac{6}{10}, \frac{9}{15}, \frac{12}{20}, \frac{15}{25}, \frac{18}{30}$
4. $\frac{12}{14}, \frac{18}{21}, \frac{24}{28}, \frac{30}{35}, \frac{36}{42}$ **5.** $\frac{14}{20}, \frac{21}{30}, \frac{28}{40}, \frac{35}{50}, \frac{42}{60}$ **6.** $\frac{8}{18}, \frac{12}{27}, \frac{16}{36}, \frac{20}{45}, \frac{24}{54}$
7. $\frac{2}{8}, \frac{3}{12}, \frac{4}{16}, \frac{5}{20}, \frac{6}{24}$ **8.** $\frac{12}{22}, \frac{18}{33}, \frac{24}{44}, \frac{30}{55}, \frac{36}{66}$ **9.** $\frac{8}{10}, \frac{12}{15}, \frac{16}{20}, \frac{20}{25}, \frac{24}{30}$
10. $\frac{10}{26}, \frac{15}{39}, \frac{20}{52}, \frac{25}{65}, \frac{30}{78}$ (Note: There are other answers possible for #1–10.) **11.** 15 **12.** 14 **13.** 11 **14.** 12 **15.** 20 **16.** 24 **17.** 32
18. 18 **19.** 9 **20.** 24 **21.** 7 **22.** 42 **23.** 18 **24.** 36 **25.** 28
26. 9 **27.** 28 **28.** 25 **29.** 66 **30.** 10

PAGE 21

1. $\frac{5}{7}$ **2.** $\frac{1}{2}$ **3.** $\frac{1}{3}$ **4.** $\frac{3}{7}$ **5.** $\frac{1}{12}$ **6.** $\frac{1}{2}$ **7.** $\frac{9}{10}$ **8.** $\frac{4}{5}$ **9.** $\frac{1}{2}$ **10.** $\frac{7}{15}$
11. $\frac{4}{7}$ **12.** $\frac{3}{7}$ **13.** $\frac{2}{5}$ **14.** $\frac{3}{4}$ **15.** $\frac{2}{5}$ **16.** $\frac{3}{4}$ **17.** $\frac{13}{15}$ **18.** $\frac{5}{12}$ **19.** $\frac{5}{6}$
20. $\frac{3}{8}$

1. $\frac{2}{10}, \frac{3}{15}, \frac{4}{20}, \frac{5}{25}, \frac{6}{30}$ 2. $\frac{8}{14}, \frac{12}{21}, \frac{16}{28}, \frac{20}{35}, \frac{24}{42}$ 3. $\frac{4}{6}, \frac{6}{9}, \frac{8}{12}, \frac{10}{15}, \frac{12}{18}$
4. $\frac{14}{16}, \frac{21}{24}, \frac{28}{32}, \frac{35}{40}, \frac{42}{48}$ 5. $\frac{2}{24}, \frac{3}{36}, \frac{4}{48}, \frac{5}{60}, \frac{6}{72}$ 6. $\frac{4}{10}, \frac{6}{15}, \frac{8}{20}, \frac{10}{25}, \frac{12}{30}$
7. $\frac{10}{18}, \frac{15}{27}, \frac{20}{36}, \frac{25}{45}, \frac{30}{54}$ 8. $\frac{10}{16}, \frac{15}{24}, \frac{20}{32}, \frac{25}{40}, \frac{30}{48}$ 9. $\frac{16}{26}, \frac{24}{39}, \frac{32}{52}, \frac{40}{65}, \frac{48}{78}$
10. $\frac{6}{8}, \frac{9}{12}, \frac{12}{16}, \frac{15}{20}, \frac{18}{24}$ (Note: There are other answers possible for
#1–10.) **11.** 3 **12.** 28 **13.** 14 **14.** 11 **15.** 28 **16.** 9 **17.** 25
18. 35 **19.** 24 **20.** 42 **21.** 9 **22.** 15 **23.** 40 **24.** 63 **25.** 35
26. 20 **27.** 21 **28.** 56 **29.** 60 **30.** 27

1. $\frac{4}{5}$ 2. $\frac{7}{8}$ 3. $\frac{1}{2}$ 4. $\frac{2}{3}$ 5. $\frac{1}{2}$ 6. $\frac{17}{18}$ 7. $\frac{4}{5}$ 8. $\frac{3}{7}$ 9. $\frac{3}{4}$ 10. $\frac{15}{16}$
11. $\frac{1}{2}$ 12. $\frac{1}{2}$ 13. $\frac{2}{3}$ 14. $\frac{1}{6}$ 15. $\frac{3}{32}$ 16. $\frac{9}{10}$ 17. $\frac{9}{10}$ 18. $\frac{2}{5}$
19. $\frac{5}{8}$ 20. $\frac{9}{10}$

1. $\frac{6}{8}, \frac{9}{12}, \frac{12}{16}, \frac{15}{20}, \frac{18}{24}$ 2. $\frac{8}{10}, \frac{12}{15}, \frac{16}{20}, \frac{20}{25}, \frac{24}{30}$ 3. $\frac{12}{14}, \frac{18}{21}, \frac{24}{28}, \frac{30}{35}, \frac{36}{42}$
4. $\frac{10}{12}, \frac{15}{18}, \frac{20}{24}, \frac{25}{30}, \frac{30}{36}$ 5. $\frac{10}{24}, \frac{15}{36}, \frac{20}{48}, \frac{25}{60}, \frac{30}{72}$ 6. $\frac{10}{16}, \frac{15}{24}, \frac{20}{32}, \frac{25}{40}, \frac{30}{48}$
7. $\frac{4}{6}, \frac{6}{9}, \frac{8}{12}, \frac{10}{15}, \frac{12}{18}$ 8. $\frac{10}{18}, \frac{15}{27}, \frac{20}{36}, \frac{25}{45}, \frac{30}{54}$ 9. $\frac{2}{4}, \frac{3}{6}, \frac{4}{8}, \frac{5}{10}, \frac{6}{12}$
10. $\frac{6}{16}, \frac{9}{24}, \frac{12}{32}, \frac{15}{40}, \frac{18}{48}$ (Note: There are other answers possible for
#1–10.) **11.** 5 **12.** 12 **13.** 45 **14.** 24 **15.** 15 **16.** 20 **17.** 28
18. 18 **19.** 12 **20.** 35 **21.** 21 **22.** 15 **23.** 21 **24.** 32 **25.** 27
26. 18 **27.** 16 **28.** 20 **29.** 20 **30.** 30

1. $\frac{2}{3}$ 2. $\frac{4}{7}$ 3. $\frac{5}{9}$ 4. $\frac{2}{3}$ 5. $\frac{9}{10}$ 6. $\frac{8}{9}$ 7. $\frac{1}{3}$ 8. $\frac{2}{3}$ 9. $\frac{3}{7}$ 10. $\frac{5}{9}$
11. $\frac{4}{5}$ 12. $\frac{2}{5}$ 13. $\frac{5}{9}$ 14. $\frac{2}{5}$ 15. $\frac{3}{5}$ 16. $\frac{4}{5}$ 17. $\frac{3}{4}$ 18. $\frac{3}{5}$ 19. $\frac{4}{7}$
20. $\frac{1}{5}$

1. 2 2. 2 3. 8 4. 4 5. 6 6. 36 7. 42 8. 27 9. 35 10. 8
11. 65 12. 44 13. 25 14. 18 15. 49 16. 7 17. 12 18. 9
19. 12 20. 45 21. 27 22. 10 23. 11 24. 9 25. 8 26. 15
27. 18 28. 39 29. 65 30. 12

1. $\frac{1}{2}$ 2. $\frac{1}{3}$ 3. $\frac{1}{4}$ 4. $\frac{1}{2}$ 5. $\frac{1}{3}$ 6. $\frac{1}{9}$ 7. $\frac{2}{3}$ 8. $\frac{2}{3}$ 9. $\frac{4}{5}$ 10. $\frac{1}{5}$
11. $\frac{1}{6}$ 12. $\frac{4}{9}$ 13. $\frac{4}{5}$ 14. $\frac{3}{5}$ 15. $\frac{2}{3}$ 16. $\frac{5}{8}$ 17. $\frac{9}{10}$ 18. $\frac{1}{2}$ 19. $\frac{2}{5}$
20. $\frac{3}{7}$ 21. $\frac{2}{3}$ 22. $\frac{3}{5}$ 23. $\frac{2}{3}$ 24. $\frac{3}{5}$ 25. $\frac{2}{3}$ 26. $\frac{3}{7}$ 27. $\frac{2}{3}$ 28. $\frac{1}{2}$
29. $\frac{3}{8}$ 30. $\frac{5}{8}$

1. 2 2. 20 3. 16 4. 9 5. 10 6. 40 7. 2 8. 15 9. 32
10. 28 11. 27 12. 65 13. 12 14. 15 15. 12 16. 9 17. 35
18. 24 19. 20 20. 15 21. 32 22. 28 23. 10 24. 28 25. 45
26. 30 27. 35 28. 40 29. 18 30. 14

1. $\frac{5}{6}$ 2. $\frac{3}{5}$ 3. $\frac{1}{3}$ 4. $\frac{2}{3}$ 5. $\frac{1}{5}$ 6. $\frac{4}{7}$ 7. $\frac{3}{8}$ 8. $\frac{4}{5}$ 9. $\frac{5}{11}$ 10. $\frac{2}{3}$
11. $\frac{2}{7}$ 12. $\frac{5}{7}$ 13. $\frac{8}{9}$ 14. $\frac{4}{7}$ 15. $\frac{1}{3}$ 16. $\frac{1}{2}$ 17. $\frac{3}{7}$ 18. $\frac{1}{8}$ 19. $\frac{1}{4}$
20. $\frac{5}{7}$ 21. $\frac{9}{11}$ 22. $\frac{3}{5}$ 23. $\frac{5}{6}$ 24. $\frac{3}{8}$ 25. $\frac{2}{3}$ 26. $\frac{1}{2}$ 27. $\frac{2}{3}$ 28. $\frac{1}{6}$
29. $\frac{3}{4}$ 30. $\frac{4}{5}$

1. 14 2. 15 3. 15 4. 12 5. 4 6. 15 7. 14 8. 10 9. 72
10. 9 11. 3 12. 20 13. 25 14. 9 15. 22 16. 16 17. 30
18. 30 19. 15 20. 21 21. 12 22. 10 23. 20 24. 18 25. 35
26. 21 27. 39 28. 4 29. 24 30. 35

1. $\frac{2}{3}$ 2. $\frac{5}{6}$ 3. $\frac{4}{15}$ 4. $\frac{3}{7}$ 5. $\frac{4}{7}$ 6. $\frac{5}{7}$ 7. $\frac{5}{8}$ 8. $\frac{5}{8}$ 9. $\frac{3}{5}$ 10. $\frac{1}{3}$
11. $\frac{6}{7}$ 12. $\frac{3}{4}$ 13. $\frac{5}{7}$ 14. $\frac{2}{3}$ 15. $\frac{5}{6}$ 16. $\frac{2}{5}$ 17. $\frac{1}{4}$ 18. $\frac{1}{12}$ 19. $\frac{2}{3}$
20. $\frac{4}{5}$ 21. $\frac{5}{6}$ 22. $\frac{2}{7}$ 23. $\frac{4}{5}$ 24. $\frac{2}{9}$ 25. $\frac{11}{13}$ 26. $\frac{7}{10}$ 27. $\frac{2}{3}$ 28. $\frac{1}{8}$
29. $\frac{2}{9}$ 30. $\frac{5}{9}$

1. 15 2. 24 3. 27 4. 30 5. 6 6. 12 7. 20 8. 33 9. 25
10. 4 11. 16 12. 36 13. 18 14. 63 15. 25 16. 16 17. 15
18. 15 19. 14 20. 15 21. 9 22. 8 23. 15 24. 32 25. 21
26. 35 27. 8 28. 8 29. 10 30. 10

1. $\frac{4}{9}$ 2. $\frac{2}{3}$ 3. $\frac{1}{2}$ 4. $\frac{2}{5}$ 5. $\frac{5}{7}$ 6. $\frac{1}{4}$ 7. $\frac{1}{2}$ 8. $\frac{11}{19}$ 9. $\frac{1}{2}$ 10. $\frac{4}{7}$
11. $\frac{3}{5}$ 12. $\frac{2}{7}$ 13. $\frac{1}{3}$ 14. $\frac{3}{7}$ 15. $\frac{7}{16}$ 16. $\frac{1}{2}$ 17. $\frac{7}{12}$ 18. $\frac{1}{8}$ 19. $\frac{1}{5}$
20. $\frac{7}{15}$ 21. $\frac{23}{32}$ 22. $\frac{1}{6}$ 23. $\frac{2}{3}$ 24. $\frac{5}{8}$ 25. $\frac{5}{12}$ 26. $\frac{2}{5}$ 27. $\frac{51}{53}$
28. $\frac{6}{7}$ 29. $\frac{5}{6}$ 30. $\frac{2}{9}$

1. 4 2. 30 3. 36 4. 33 5. 24 6. 18 7. 3 8. 10 9. 35
10. 18 11. 21 12. 30 13. 21 14. 16 15. 16 16. 42 17. 45
18. 36 19. 28 20. 25 21. 25 22. 18 23. 32 24. 25 25. 35
26. 21 27. 55 28. 16 29. 16 30. 28

1. $\frac{1}{2}$ 2. $\frac{2}{5}$ 3. $\frac{1}{6}$ 4. $\frac{6}{7}$ 5. $\frac{1}{9}$ 6. $\frac{1}{4}$ 7. $\frac{1}{3}$ 8. $\frac{7}{9}$ 9. $\frac{4}{9}$ 10. $\frac{3}{5}$
11. $\frac{2}{3}$ 12. $\frac{1}{6}$ 13. $\frac{3}{19}$ 14. $\frac{2}{3}$ 15. $\frac{7}{13}$ 16. $\frac{2}{7}$ 17. $\frac{2}{5}$ 18. $\frac{1}{7}$ 19. $\frac{6}{7}$
20. $\frac{5}{9}$ 21. $\frac{3}{4}$ 22. $\frac{3}{7}$ 23. $\frac{4}{5}$ 24. $\frac{4}{7}$ 25. $\frac{1}{3}$ 26. $\frac{2}{5}$ 27. $\frac{2}{5}$ 28. $\frac{2}{9}$
29. $\frac{7}{9}$ 30. $\frac{5}{8}$

1. = 2. = 3. ≠ 4. ≠ 5. ≠ 6. ≠ 7. ≠ 8. = 9. ≠ 10. =
11. ≠ 12. ≠ 13. 9 14. 2 15. 36 16. 14 17. 20 18. 6
19. 21 20. 5 21. 28 22. 24 23. 138 24. 150

1. 1,125 km   **2.** 30 feet   **3.** $756/mo   **4.** 1,350 square feet

PAGE 38
1. ≠   **2.** ≠   **3.** =   **4.** =   **5.** ≠   **6.** =   **7.** =   **8.** ≠   **9.** ≠   **10.** ≠
11. =   **12.** =   **13.** 12   **14.** 20   **15.** 187   **16.** 156   **17.** 6   **18.** 46
19. 69   **20.** 26   **21.** 21   **22.** 6   **23.** 10   **24.** 5

PAGE 39
1. 48,000   **2.** 72 inches   **3.** $408   **4.** 16

PAGE 40
1. =   **2.** ≠   **3.** =   **4.** ≠   **5.** ≠   **6.** =   **7.** =   **8.** ≠   **9.** ≠   **10.** =
11. =   **12.** ≠   **13.** 10   **14.** 88   **15.** 54   **16.** 24   **17.** 75   **18.** 39
19. 45   **20.** 51   **21.** 52   **22.** 10   **23.** 57   **24.** 12

PAGE 41
1. 16   **2.** 297 cents   **3.** 210 miles   **4.** 39 in.

PAGE 42
1. =   **2.** =   **3.** ≠   **4.** ≠   **5.** =   **6.** ≠   **7.** =   **8.** ≠   **9.** ≠   **10.** =
11. ≠   **12.** =   **13.** 104   **14.** 78   **15.** 91   **16.** 117   **17.** 24
18. 221   **19.** 105   **20.** 38   **21.** 69   **22.** 64   **23.** 4   **24.** 16

PAGE 43
1. 6 hours   **2.** 52 feet   **3.** 45 dozen   **4.** 4

PAGE 44
1. =   **2.** ≠   **3.** =   **4.** ≠   **5.** ≠   **6.** =   **7.** =   **8.** ≠   **9.** ≠   **10.** =
11. ≠   **12.** =   **13.** 20   **14.** 20   **15.** 3   **16.** 15   **17.** 42   **18.** 4
19. 36   **20.** 180   **21.** 6   **22.** 7   **23.** 60   **24.** 5

PAGE 45
1. 48 feet   **2.** 348 cents   **3.** 25 hours   **4.** 12

PAGE 49
1. 20   **2.** 36   **3.** 35   **4.** 42   **5.** 60   **6.** 20   **7.** 6   **8.** 18   **9.** 48
10. 140   **11.** 176   **12.** 54   **13.** 42   **14.** 80   **15.** 150   **16.** 120
17. 120   **18.** 140   **19.** 30   **20.** 108   **21.** 210   **22.** 110   **23.** 160
24. 144

PAGE 50
1. $\frac{1}{3}$ **2.** $\frac{1}{4}$ **3.** $\frac{2}{8}$ **4.** $\frac{9}{16}$ **5.** $\frac{4}{5}$ **6.** $\frac{1}{3}$ **7.** $\frac{1}{5}$ **8.** $\frac{2}{16}$ **9.** $\frac{2}{7}$ **10.** $\frac{3}{7}$
11. $\frac{9}{14}$ **12.** $\frac{5}{10}$ **13.** $\frac{5}{9}$ **14.** $\frac{15}{20}$ **15.** $\frac{2}{3}$ **16.** $\frac{3}{4}$ **17.** $\frac{3}{8}$ **18.** $\frac{1}{4}$
19. $\frac{2}{9}$ **20.** $\frac{4}{9}$ **21.** $\frac{5}{8}$ **22.** $\frac{4}{7}$ **23.** $\frac{5}{16}$ **24.** $\frac{2}{5}$ **25.** $\frac{7}{8}$ **26.** $\frac{1}{9}$ **27.** $\frac{5}{12}$
28. $\frac{7}{15}$ **29.** $\frac{3}{16}$ **30.** $\frac{7}{13}$

PAGE 51
1. 6   **2.** 15   **3.** 24   **4.** 12   **5.** 30   **6.** 80   **7.** 4   **8.** 12   **9.** 80
10. 60   **11.** 90   **12.** 45   **13.** 6   **14.** 8   **15.** 90   **16.** 28   **17.** 40
18. 36   **19.** 24   **20.** 36   **21.** 60   **22.** 75   **23.** 72   **24.** 175

PAGE 52
1. $\frac{13}{22}$ **2.** $\frac{2}{3}$ **3.** $\frac{1}{3}$ **4.** $\frac{4}{9}$ **5.** $\frac{7}{12}$ **6.** $\frac{1}{8}$ **7.** $\frac{1}{3}$ **8.** $\frac{3}{7}$ **9.** $\frac{7}{20}$ **10.** $\frac{1}{2}$
11. $\frac{5}{16}$ **12.** $\frac{7}{15}$ **13.** $\frac{7}{10}$ **14.** $\frac{31}{64}$ **15.** $\frac{5}{6}$ **16.** $\frac{3}{11}$ **17.** $\frac{1}{7}$ **18.** $\frac{5}{13}$
19. $\frac{1}{4}$ **20.** $\frac{4}{9}$ **21.** $\frac{17}{36}$ **22.** $\frac{11}{100}$ **23.** $\frac{1}{2}$ **24.** $\frac{3}{50}$ **25.** $\frac{11}{13}$ **26.** $\frac{1}{3}$
27. $\frac{7}{18}$ **28.** $\frac{7}{12}$ **29.** $\frac{4}{15}$ **30.** $\frac{5}{12}$

PAGE 53
1. 12   **2.** 39   **3.** 64   **4.** 20   **5.** 30   **6.** 150   **7.** 35   **8.** 102   **9.** 9
10. 45   **11.** 44   **12.** 48   **13.** 60   **14.** 66   **15.** 85   **16.** 60   **17.** 32
18. 15   **19.** 80   **20.** 21   **21.** 91   **22.** 16   **23.** 60   **24.** 104

PAGE 54
1. $\frac{20}{57}$ **2.** $\frac{15}{24}$ **3.** $\frac{9}{12}$ **4.** $\frac{7}{13}$ **5.** $\frac{15}{20}$ **6.** $\frac{2}{3}$ **7.** $\frac{1}{10}$ **8.** $\frac{3}{4}$ **9.** $\frac{2}{9}$
10. $\frac{3}{20}$ **11.** $\frac{3}{12}$ **12.** $\frac{7}{15}$ **13.** $\frac{2}{12}$ **14.** $\frac{8}{24}$ **15.** $\frac{5}{7}$ **16.** $\frac{3}{8}$ **17.** $\frac{3}{8}$
18. $\frac{3}{10}$ **19.** $\frac{5}{16}$ **20.** $\frac{4}{15}$ **21.** $\frac{4}{9}$ **22.** $\frac{7}{9}$ **23.** $\frac{8}{21}$ **24.** $\frac{13}{18}$ **25.** $\frac{15}{24}$
26. $\frac{7}{16}$ **27.** $\frac{7}{9}$ **28.** $\frac{11}{16}$ **29.** $\frac{7}{15}$ **30.** $\frac{4}{5}$

PAGE 55
1. 14   **2.** 160   **3.** 180   **4.** 56   **5.** 24   **6.** 30   **7.** 56   **8.** 100
9. 231   **10.** 60   **11.** 60   **12.** 60   **13.** 189   **14.** 50   **15.** 39
16. 42   **17.** 48   **18.** 16   **19.** 360   **20.** 48   **21.** 51   **22.** 36
23. 45   **24.** 12

PAGE 56
1. $\frac{9}{26}$ **2.** $\frac{1}{5}$ **3.** $\frac{3}{5}$ **4.** $\frac{2}{3}$ **5.** $\frac{3}{8}$ **6.** $\frac{1}{14}$ **7.** $\frac{5}{16}$ **8.** $\frac{4}{7}$ **9.** $\frac{3}{7}$ **10.** $\frac{11}{20}$
11. $\frac{7}{25}$ **12.** $\frac{1}{5}$ **13.** $\frac{1}{4}$ **14.** $\frac{11}{16}$ **15.** $\frac{5}{12}$ **16.** $\frac{4}{7}$ **17.** $\frac{3}{5}$ **18.** $\frac{3}{5}$
19. $\frac{7}{9}$ **20.** $\frac{5}{13}$ **21.** $\frac{17}{36}$ **22.** $\frac{5}{16}$ **23.** $\frac{5}{16}$ **24.** $\frac{3}{7}$ **25.** $\frac{9}{13}$ **26.** $\frac{7}{10}$
27. $\frac{3}{5}$ **28.** $\frac{11}{26}$ **29.** $\frac{8}{9}$ **30.** $\frac{7}{12}$

PAGE 57
1. 6   **2.** 18   **3.** 24   **4.** 104   **5.** 20   **6.** 30   **7.** 6   **8.** 16   **9.** 24
10. 44   **11.** 48   **12.** 52   **13.** 15   **14.** 12   **15.** 35   **16.** 50   **17.** 25
18. 36   **19.** 48   **20.** 15   **21.** 30   **22.** 32   **23.** 33   **24.** 27

PAGE 58
1. $\frac{9}{16}$ **2.** $\frac{7}{15}$ **3.** $\frac{1}{4}$ **4.** $\frac{4}{5}$ **5.** $\frac{3}{8}$ **6.** $\frac{1}{4}$ **7.** $\frac{1}{10}$ **8.** $\frac{2}{3}$ **9.** $\frac{2}{11}$ **10.** $\frac{5}{9}$
11. $\frac{9}{14}$ **12.** $\frac{1}{2}$ **13.** $\frac{1}{5}$ **14.** $\frac{3}{5}$ **15.** $\frac{5}{16}$ **16.** $\frac{7}{15}$ **17.** $\frac{3}{16}$ **18.** $\frac{3}{8}$
19. $\frac{7}{10}$ **20.** $\frac{5}{8}$ **21.** $\frac{15}{20}$ **22.** $\frac{1}{2}$ **23.** $\frac{7}{8}$ **24.** $\frac{5}{8}$ **25.** $\frac{13}{18}$ **26.** $\frac{6}{11}$
27. $\frac{5}{12}$ **28.** $\frac{5}{8}$ **29.** $\frac{11}{21}$ **30.** $\frac{11}{13}$

PAGE 59

1. $1\frac{3}{16}$ 2. $1\frac{6}{17}$ 3. $1\frac{13}{15}$ 4. $2\frac{4}{17}$ 5. $1\frac{17}{18}$ 6. $2\frac{2}{19}$ 7. $1\frac{7}{29}$ 8. $1\frac{19}{31}$
9. $2\frac{9}{17}$ 10. $2\frac{2}{35}$ 11. $1\frac{7}{8}$ 12. $1\frac{7}{9}$ 13. $\frac{7}{4}$ 14. $\frac{85}{8}$ 15. $\frac{13}{2}$ 16. $\frac{26}{3}$
17. $\frac{46}{5}$ 18. $\frac{28}{5}$ 19. $\frac{20}{3}$ 20. $\frac{43}{5}$ 21. $\frac{19}{3}$ 22. $\frac{23}{4}$ 23. $\frac{5}{2}$ 24. $\frac{73}{8}$

PAGE 60

1. $7\frac{4}{9}$ 2. $14\frac{1}{2}$ 3. $8\frac{1}{5}$ 4. $11\frac{1}{2}$ 5. $8\frac{1}{3}$ 6. 20 7. $14\frac{1}{2}$ 8. $11\frac{2}{3}$
9. $9\frac{1}{2}$ 10. $7\frac{1}{2}$ 11. $14\frac{1}{4}$ 12. $9\frac{2}{7}$ 13. $10\frac{1}{2}$ 14. $8\frac{1}{4}$ 15. 14
16. $5\frac{1}{8}$

PAGE 61

1. $1\frac{1}{2}$ 2. $3\frac{7}{10}$ 3. $2\frac{4}{47}$ 4. $2\frac{8}{33}$ 5. $2\frac{7}{20}$ 6. $2\frac{1}{19}$ 7. $1\frac{23}{32}$ 8. $8\frac{3}{4}$
9. $3\frac{5}{8}$ 10. $4\frac{2}{13}$ 11. $2\frac{4}{7}$ 12. $2\frac{7}{11}$ 13. $\frac{35}{6}$ 14. $\frac{67}{9}$ 15. $\frac{87}{7}$ 16. $\frac{53}{8}$
17. $\frac{43}{9}$ 18. $\frac{31}{2}$ 19. $\frac{39}{5}$ 20. $\frac{27}{8}$ 21. $\frac{11}{4}$ 22. $\frac{14}{3}$ 23. $\frac{83}{5}$ 24. $\frac{29}{6}$

PAGE 62

1. $8\frac{1}{6}$ 2. $18\frac{1}{3}$ 3. $5\frac{1}{3}$ 4. $17\frac{1}{3}$ 5. $7\frac{3}{4}$ 6. $51\frac{1}{5}$ 7. 18 8. $9\frac{1}{4}$
9. $20\frac{1}{2}$ 10. $18\frac{2}{5}$ 11. $6\frac{2}{5}$ 12. $10\frac{1}{2}$ 13. $30\frac{4}{5}$ 14. $16\frac{1}{2}$ 15. $15\frac{1}{3}$
16. $16\frac{4}{11}$

PAGE 63

1. $8\frac{1}{25}$ 2. $17\frac{5}{9}$ 3. $2\frac{2}{65}$ 4. $3\frac{1}{3}$ 5. $2\frac{7}{16}$ 6. $10\frac{5}{11}$ 7. $6\frac{8}{15}$ 8. $3\frac{5}{14}$
9. $16\frac{2}{5}$ 10. $29\frac{3}{4}$ 11. $22\frac{1}{3}$ 12. $160\frac{1}{3}$ 13. $\frac{39}{5}$ 14. $\frac{39}{8}$ 15. $\frac{36}{5}$
16. $\frac{75}{8}$ 17. $\frac{43}{9}$ 18. $\frac{31}{2}$ 19. $\frac{23}{5}$ 20. $\frac{53}{8}$ 21. $\frac{31}{11}$ 22. $\frac{61}{8}$ 23. $\frac{51}{4}$
24. $\frac{7}{2}$

PAGE 64

1. $54\frac{1}{2}$ 2. $4\frac{4}{5}$ 3. $17\frac{1}{3}$ 4. $27\frac{1}{4}$ 5. $14\frac{1}{2}$ 6. $9\frac{1}{3}$ 7. $14\frac{4}{5}$ 8. $17\frac{3}{4}$
9. $26\frac{11}{14}$ 10. $28\frac{1}{6}$ 11. $15\frac{1}{6}$ 12. $13\frac{2}{7}$ 13. 11 14. $39\frac{1}{4}$ 15. $12\frac{4}{5}$
16. $17\frac{1}{2}$

PAGE 65

1. $34\frac{2}{5}$ 2. $47\frac{1}{6}$ 3. $21\frac{6}{25}$ 4. $72\frac{2}{5}$ 5. $45\frac{1}{8}$ 6. $27\frac{3}{10}$ 7. $4\frac{3}{14}$
8. $16\frac{22}{23}$ 9. $38\frac{13}{15}$ 10. $60\frac{11}{12}$ 11. $29\frac{1}{5}$ 12. $28\frac{7}{8}$ 13. $\frac{64}{9}$ 14. $\frac{34}{5}$
15. $\frac{29}{3}$ 16. $\frac{51}{8}$ 17. $\frac{12}{5}$ 18. $\frac{56}{5}$ 19. $\frac{23}{4}$ 20. $\frac{61}{9}$ 21. $\frac{27}{2}$ 22. $\frac{71}{3}$
23. $\frac{131}{16}$ 24. $\frac{55}{12}$

PAGE 66

1. $9\frac{1}{4}$ 2. $22\frac{6}{5}$ 3. $15\frac{2}{5}$ 4. $9\frac{2}{5}$ 5. 10 6. $4\frac{11}{18}$ 7. 7 8. $35\frac{4}{9}$
9. $20\frac{1}{3}$ 10. $5\frac{1}{2}$ 11. $15\frac{3}{4}$ 12. $39\frac{1}{4}$ 13. $15\frac{1}{2}$ 14. 8 15. 52
16. $19\frac{1}{3}$

PAGE 67

1. $25\frac{4}{5}$ 2. 23 3. $21\frac{5}{7}$ 4. $36\frac{5}{8}$ 5. $54\frac{3}{5}$ 6. $5\frac{1}{30}$ 7. $14\frac{12}{25}$ 8. $44\frac{1}{3}$
9. $21\frac{8}{13}$ 10. $26\frac{2}{15}$ 11. $10\frac{12}{13}$ 12. $21\frac{2}{11}$ 13. $\frac{33}{5}$ 14. $\frac{23}{9}$ 15. $\frac{41}{6}$
16. $\frac{11}{3}$ 17. $\frac{41}{4}$ 18. $\frac{43}{4}$ 19. $\frac{13}{2}$ 20. $\frac{24}{7}$ 21. $\frac{19}{3}$ 22. $\frac{113}{9}$ 23. $\frac{68}{9}$
24. $\frac{51}{4}$

PAGE 68

1. $7\frac{2}{5}$ 2. $4\frac{1}{2}$ 3. $14\frac{1}{2}$ 4. $15\frac{1}{4}$ 5. $8\frac{4}{5}$ 6. $11\frac{5}{7}$ 7. $9\frac{1}{7}$ 8. $16\frac{1}{4}$
9. $3\frac{1}{2}$ 10. $5\frac{1}{3}$ 11. $14\frac{5}{6}$ 12. $19\frac{1}{3}$ 13. $13\frac{1}{2}$ 14. 6 15. $13\frac{1}{3}$
16. $5\frac{4}{5}$

PAGE 75

1. eight tenths 2. twenty-seven and four tenths 3. six and two hundred thirty-four thousandths 4. five hundred ten and sixty-one hundredths 5. thirty-nine and five hundred twenty-seven thousandths 6. four thousand two and seven tenths 7. seventy-four thousand six hundred twenty-one and twenty-eight hundredths 8. eighty and nine hundredths 9. seven and three hundred twenty-five thousandths 10. two hundred fifty-six and forty-nine hundredths

PAGE 76

1. 0.7 2. 0.42 3. 5.6 4. 105.057 5. 2,008.4 6. 27.405
7. 37.021 8. 4,052.11 9. 14.58 10. 217.083

PAGE 77

1. thirty-five hundredths 2. forty-two and seven tenths 3. two hundred six and four tenths 4. eighty-five and twenty-one hundredths 5. three hundred twelve and six hundredths 6. forty-three and five thousandths 7. eight thousand two hundred twenty and one tenth 8. fifty-nine and eight tenths 9. four and thirty-five thousandths 10. ninety-one and fifty-seven hundredths

PAGE 78

1. 53.2 2. 607.05 3. 8.0421 4. 66.005 5. 2,803.59
6. 672.4343 7. 76,095.2 8. 861.72 9. 9.507 10. 23.84

PAGE 79

1. twenty-three and eight tenths 2. four hundred six and fifty-nine hundredths 3. nine and two hundred seven thousandths 4. fifty-six and three thousand five ten thousandths 5. six thousand two hundred eighteen and six tenths 6. seventeen and two hundredths 7. two hundred forty-three and one hundred nine thousandths 8. sixty-seven thousand two hundred nine and four tenths 9. sixty-two and ninety-one hundredths 10. five and three hundred seventy-five thousandths

PAGE 80

1. 4.29 2. 0.602 3. 95.416 4. 407.32 5. 2,561.008 6. 75.2
7. 906.43 8. 2,074.05 9. 29.32 10. 60,157.0209

PAGE 81

1. forty-three and twenty-six hundredths **2.** five hundred seventy-two thousandths **3.** twenty-eight and nine hundred six thousandths **4.** four hundred seventeen and twenty-eight hundredths **5.** five hundred twelve thousandths **6.** sixty-seven and forty-three hundredths **7.** two hundred five and three tenths **8.** fifty-six thousand four hundred thirty-two and five hundredths **9.** two hundred seventy-three and ninety-two hundredths **10.** seventy-eight and seven tenths

PAGE 82

1. 0.56 **2.** 29.321 **3.** 806.93 **4.** 5,741.02 **5.** 96.75 **6.** 4.3 **7.** 879.562 **8.** 67.3 **9.** 0.57 **10.** 93,418.27

PAGE 83

1. twenty-six and three tenths **2.** ninety-five hundredths **3.** six thousand seventy-one and twenty-nine hundredths **4.** four hundred thirty-five and six hundred thirty-one thousandths **5.** forty-three thousand two hundred seventeen and four tenths **6.** six hundred six and seven hundred seven thousandths **7.** five hundred thirty-one and two hundred fifteen thousandths **8.** thirty-nine and five tenths **9.** fifty-eight and two tenths **10.** nine hundred forty and seventy-two hundredths

PAGE 84

1. 92.5 **2.** 6.714 **3.** 80.32 **4.** 9.2 **5.** 0.95 **6.** 832.67 **7.** 43,201.2 **8.** 575.31 **9.** 0.7005 **10.** 69.52

PAGE 85

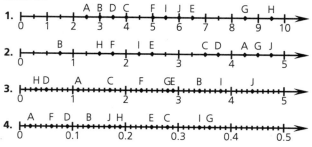

PAGE 86

1. A: $\frac{1}{3}$; B: 1; C: $1\frac{1}{3}$; D: $1\frac{2}{3}$; E: 2; F: 3; G: $3\frac{1}{3}$; H: $3\frac{2}{3}$; I: 4; J: $4\frac{2}{3}$
2. A: 0.02; B: 0.09; C: 0.16; D: 0.19: E: 0.26; F: 0.28; G: 0.3; H: 0.36; I: 0.4; J: 0.49

PAGE 87

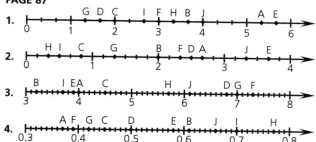

PAGE 88

1. A: $\frac{3}{5}$; B: $1\frac{2}{5}$; C: $1\frac{4}{5}$; D: $2\frac{2}{5}$; E: 3; F: $3\frac{3}{5}$; G: $3\frac{4}{5}$; H: $4\frac{1}{5}$; I: 5; J: $5\frac{3}{5}$
2. A: 0.002; B: 0.008; C: 0.011; D: 0.016; E: 0.023; F: 0.027; G: 0.032; H: 0.037; I: 0.041; J: 0.047

PAGE 89

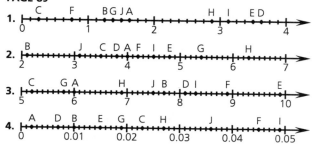

PAGE 90

1. A: $2\frac{1}{4}$; B: $2\frac{3}{4}$; C: $3\frac{1}{2}$; D: $3\frac{3}{4}$; E: $4\frac{1}{4}$; F: $4\frac{3}{4}$; G: 5; H: $5\frac{1}{2}$; I: $6\frac{1}{4}$; J: $6\frac{3}{4}$
2. A: 0.53; B: 0.57; C: 0.62; D: 0.7; E: 0.74; F: 0.81; G: 0.85; H: 0.89; I: 0.93; J: 1

PAGE 91

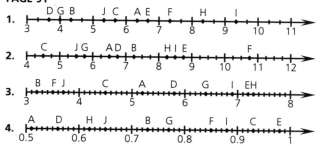

PAGE 92

1. A: $4\frac{3}{8}$; B: $4\frac{7}{8}$; C: $5\frac{1}{8}$; D: $5\frac{5}{8}$; E: 6; F: $6\frac{1}{2}$; G: 7; H: $7\frac{1}{8}$; I: $7\frac{5}{8}$; J: 8
2. A: 0.003; B: 0.009; C: 0.017; D: 0.024; E: 0.026; F: 0.032; G: 0.038; H: 0.042; I: 0.047; J: 0.05

PAGE 93

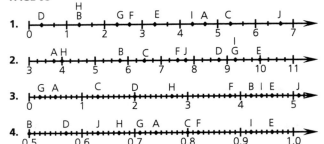

PAGE 94

1. A: $4\frac{1}{4}$; B: $4\frac{5}{8}$; C: 5; D: $5\frac{3}{8}$; E: $5\frac{1}{2}$; F: $6\frac{1}{8}$; G: $6\frac{3}{8}$; H: $6\frac{7}{8}$; I: $7\frac{1}{4}$; J: $7\frac{1}{2}$

2. A: 0.002; B: 0.004; C: 0.009; D: 0.013; E: 0.02; F: 0.025;

G: 0.031; H: 0.035; I: 0.038; J: 0.047

PAGE 95

1. 0.5　**2.** 0.25　**3.** $0.41\overline{6}$　**4.** $0.2\overline{6}$　**5.** 0.35　**6.** $0.4\overline{5}$　**7.** 0.375

8. 0.1875　**9.** $0.291\overline{6}$　**10.** 0.3　**11.** 0.38　**12.** $0.\overline{285714}$

13. 0.15625　**14.** $0.\overline{3}$　**15.** $0.3\overline{18}$　**16.** $0.\overline{1}$　**17.** 0.4　**18.** 0.75

19. 0.8　**20.** 0.7

PAGE 96

1. $\frac{1}{5}$　**2.** $\frac{9}{10}$　**3.** $\frac{3}{8}$　**4.** $\frac{4}{5}$　**5.** $\frac{21}{50}$　**6.** $\frac{1}{2}$　**7.** $\frac{5}{32}$　**8.** $\frac{43}{100}$　**9.** $\frac{3}{16}$

10. $\frac{7}{10}$　**11.** $\frac{13}{20}$　**12.** $\frac{1}{4}$　**13.** $\frac{4}{25}$　**14.** $\frac{3}{10}$　**15.** $\frac{2}{5}$　**16.** $\frac{61}{200}$　**17.** $\frac{7}{20}$

18. $\frac{23}{200}$　**19.** $\frac{3}{4}$　**20.** $\frac{3}{25}$

PAGE 97

1. 0.1　**2.** $0.\overline{7}$　**3.** $0.8\overline{3}$　**4.** 0.34375　**5.** $0.\overline{6}$　**6.** $0.\overline{142857}$

7. 0.4375　**8.** 0.6　**9.** $0.\overline{4}$　**10.** $0.0\overline{9}$　**11.** 0.5　**12.** 0.12

13. 0.125　**14.** $0.208\overline{3}$　**15.** 0.75　**16.** $0.4\overline{6}$　**17.** 0.45

18. $0.\overline{714285}$　**19.** $0.1\overline{36}$　**20.** $0.0\overline{5}$

PAGE 98

1. $\frac{3}{4}$　**2.** $\frac{3}{5}$　**3.** $\frac{1}{8}$　**4.** $\frac{1}{10}$　**5.** $\frac{3}{20}$　**6.** $\frac{1}{2}$　**7.** $\frac{29}{40}$　**8.** $\frac{21}{25}$　**9.** $\frac{7}{16}$　**10.** $\frac{8}{25}$

11. $\frac{9}{20}$　**12.** $\frac{7}{50}$　**13.** $\frac{3}{25}$　**14.** $\frac{67}{100}$　**15.** $\frac{19}{20}$　**16.** $\frac{23}{50}$　**17.** $\frac{7}{25}$　**18.** $\frac{9}{10}$

19. $\frac{7}{8}$　**20.** $\frac{1}{4}$

PAGE 99

1. 0.75　**2.** 0.28　**3.** 0.5　**4.** $0.\overline{5}$　**5.** 0.45　**6.** $0.\overline{27}$　**7.** $0.13\overline{8}$

8. 0.21875　**9.** $0.\overline{185}$　**10.** $0.\overline{3}$　**11.** $0.2\overline{27}$　**12.** 0.2　**13.** $0.208\overline{3}$

14. 0.9　**15.** $0.\overline{571428}$　**16.** $0.58\overline{3}$　**17.** 0.875　**18.** $0.0\overline{6}$　**19.** $0.\overline{21}$

20. $0.2\overline{3}$

PAGE 100

1. $\frac{1}{4}$　**2.** $\frac{4}{5}$　**3.** $\frac{7}{10}$　**4.** $\frac{3}{25}$　**5.** $\frac{6}{25}$　**6.** $\frac{3}{16}$　**7.** $\frac{91}{100}$　**8.** $\frac{1}{2}$　**9.** $\frac{31}{50}$

10. $\frac{5}{8}$　**11.** $\frac{1}{20}$　**12.** $\frac{43}{200}$　**13.** $\frac{33}{50}$　**14.** $\frac{7}{20}$　**15.** $\frac{27}{200}$　**16.** $\frac{9}{50}$

17. $\frac{123}{200}$　**18.** $\frac{1}{25}$　**19.** $\frac{3}{80}$　**20.** $\frac{1}{100}$

PAGE 101

1. 0.8　**2.** $0.\overline{428571}$　**3.** 0.12　**4.** $0.1\overline{6}$　**5.** 0.25　**6.** $0.58\overline{3}$　**7.** $0.\overline{8}$

8. 0.1875　**9.** $0.\overline{15}$　**10.** $0.2\overline{7}$　**11.** 0.7　**12.** 0.625　**13.** $0.\overline{2}$

14. 0.35　**15.** 0.5　**16.** 0.28125　**17.** $0.\overline{90}$　**18.** $0.\overline{6}$　**19.** $0.7\overline{3}$

20. $0.\overline{857142}$

PAGE 102

1. $\frac{9}{10}$　**2.** $\frac{1}{2}$　**3.** $\frac{19}{50}$　**4.** $\frac{7}{200}$　**5.** $\frac{3}{4}$　**6.** $\frac{16}{25}$　**7.** $\frac{9}{20}$　**8.** $\frac{22}{25}$　**9.** $\frac{1}{5}$

10. $\frac{3}{40}$　**11.** $\frac{2}{25}$　**12.** $\frac{7}{32}$　**13.** $\frac{17}{20}$　**14.** $\frac{9}{25}$　**15.** $\frac{3}{8}$　**16.** $\frac{3}{10}$　**17.** $\frac{9}{100}$

18. $\frac{19}{200}$　**19.** $\frac{87}{100}$　**20.** $\frac{24}{25}$

PAGE 103

1. 0.2　**2.** $0.41\overline{6}$　**3.** $0.\overline{7}$　**4.** 0.28125　**5.** 0.75　**6.** $0.\overline{8}$　**7.** 0.0625

8. $0.\overline{428571}$　**9.** $0.\overline{6}$　**10.** 0.5625　**11.** 0.3　**12.** $0.\overline{714285}$　**13.** 0.5

14. 0.625　**15.** 0.6　**16.** 0.21875　**17.** $0.458\overline{3}$　**18.** 0.15　**19.** 0.24

20. $0.3\overline{18}$

PAGE 104

1. $\frac{1}{10}$　**2.** $\frac{67}{100}$　**3.** $\frac{21}{25}$　**4.** $\frac{1}{4}$　**5.** $\frac{1}{100}$　**6.** $\frac{1}{2}$　**7.** $\frac{5}{8}$　**8.** $\frac{33}{100}$　**9.** $\frac{7}{16}$

10. $\frac{9}{25}$　**11.** $\frac{7}{50}$　**12.** $\frac{1}{40}$　**13.** $\frac{3}{10}$　**14.** $\frac{1}{8}$　**15.** $\frac{9}{20}$　**16.** $\frac{9}{100}$　**17.** $\frac{3}{16}$

18. $\frac{3}{5}$　**19.** $\frac{61}{200}$　**20.** $\frac{3}{4}$